THE
HEART OF BUDDHISM

BEING
AN ANTHOLOGY OF BUDDHIST VERSE

THE HERITAGE OF INDIA

THE HEART OF BUDDHISM

BEING

AN ANTHOLOGY OF BUDDHIST VERSE

TRANSLATED AND EDITED BY

K. J. SAUNDERS, M. A.

LITERARY SECRETARY OF THE Y.M.C.A. OF INDIA
BURMA AND CEYLON
EDITOR AND JOINT-TRANSLATOR OF THE
'DHAMMAPADA IN THE 'WISDOM OF THE EAST' SERIES

GYAN

Published by

Gyan Publishing House
5, Ansari Road
Daryaganj, New Delhi-110002
Phone: 011-47034999, 9811692060
E-mail: books@gyanbooks.com

Distribution Network
gyanbooks.com
India, USA, Canada, UK, Australia, France

ISBN : 978-81-212-3475-7 (PB)
First Published, 1915

2nd Impression 2020

Printed at: Gyan Press, Delhi.

The Heart of Buddhism
Author: K. J. Saunders, M.A.

THE HERITAGE OF INDIA

Joint Editors. { The Right Reverend V. S. Azariah, Bishop of Dornakal.
J. N. Farquhar, M.A.

Subjects proposed and volumes under preparation.

SANSKRIT AND PALI LITERATURE.

Hymns from the Vedas. Prof. A. A. Macdonell, Oxford.

Anthology of Mahāyāna Literature. Prof. L. de la Vallée Poussin, Ghent.

Selections from the Upanishads.

Scenes from the *Rāmāyaṇa*.

Selections from the *Mahābhārata*.

THE PHILOSOPHIES.

The Sāṅkhya System. Prof. A. Berriedale Keith, Edinburgh.

The Philosophy of the Upanishads.

Śaṅkara's Vedānta. N. C. Mukerji, M.A., Allahabad.

Rāmānuja's Vedānta.

The Buddhist System.

FINE ART AND MUSIC.

Indian Painting. Principal Percy Brown, Calcutta.

Indian Architecture. R. L. Ewing, B.A., Madras.

Indian Sculpture. Principal W. M. Zumbro, Madura.

The Minor Arts. Principal Percy Brown, Calcutta.

Indian Coins.

BIOGRAPHIES OF EMINENT INDIANS.

Gautama Buddha. K. J. SAUNDERS, M.A., Rangoon.

Aśoka. J. M. MACPHAIL, M.A., M.D., Bamdah.

Śaṅkara.

Rāmānuja.

Akbar. D. E. EVANS, B.A., Mirzapore.

Tulsī Dās. S. K. DUTTA, B.A., M.B., Ch.B., Lahore.

VERNACULAR LITERATURE.

The Kurraḷ. H. A. POPLEY, B.A., Erode.

Hymns of the Aḍiyārs. G. E. PHILLIPS, M.A., and FRANCIS KINGSBURY, Bangalore.

Hymns of the Āḷvārs.

Māṇikka Vāchakar.

Tāyumānavar. ISAAC TAMBYAH, M.A., Bar.-at-Law, Penang.

Hymns of Hindustan.

Chaitanya Hymns.

Marāthī Abhaṅgs.

Gujarātī Hymns.

Sinhalese Literature. H. S. PERERA, B.A., Kandy.

HISTORIES OF VERNACULAR LITERATURE.

Bengālī. C. S. PATERSON, M.A., Calcutta.

Gujarātī.

Hindī. EDWIN GREAVES, Benares.

Kanarese. E. P. RICE, B.A., Bangalore.

Marāthī.

Tamil.

Telugu.

EDITORIAL PREFACE

> Finally, brethren, whatsoever things are true, whatsoever things are honourable, whatsoever things are just, whatsoever things are pure, whatsoever things are lovely, whatsoever things are of good report; if there be any virtue, and if there be any praise, think on these things.

No section of the population of India can afford to neglect her ancient heritage. In her literature, philosophy, art, and regulated life there is much that is worthless, much also that is distinctly unhealthy; yet the treasures of knowledge, wisdom, and beauty which they contain are too precious to be lost. Every citizen of India needs to use them, if he is to be a cultured modern Indian. This is as true of the Christian, the Muslim, the Zoroastrian as of the Hindu. But, while the heritage of India has been largely explored by scholars, and the results of their toil are laid out for us in their books, they cannot be said to be really available for the ordinary man. The volumes are in most cases expensive, and are often technical and difficult. Hence this series of cheap books has been planned by a group of Christian men, in order that every educated Indian, whether rich or poor, may be able to find his way into the treasures of India's past. Many Europeans, both in India and elsewhere, will doubtless be glad to use the series.

The utmost care is being taken by the General Editors in selecting writers, and in passing manuscripts for the press. To every book two tests are rigidly applied: everything must be scholarly, and everything must be sympathetic. The purpose is to bring the best out of the ancient treasuries, so that it may be known, enjoyed, and used.

BHIKKHUS ON THEIR BEGGING-ROUNDS

'Downcast their eyes ; their paces measured, sober . .' (p. 29)

Photograph by *Samuel Brothers, Rangoon*

Frontispiece

THE HERITAGE OF INDIA

THE HEART OF BUDDHISM

BEING

AN ANTHOLOGY OF BUDDHIST VERSE

TRANSLATED AND EDITED BY

K. J. SAUNDERS, M.A.

LITERARY SECRETARY OF THE Y.M.C.A. OF INDIA
BURMA AND CEYLON
EDITOR AND JOINT-TRANSLATOR OF THE 'DHAMMAPADA
IN THE 'WISDOM OF THE EAST' SERIES

HUMPHREY MILFORD
OXFORD UNIVERSITY PRESS
LONDON, NEW YORK, TORONTO, MELBOURNE
BOMBAY AND MADRAS
THE ASSOCIATION PRESS
86 COLLEGE STREET, CALCUTTA
1915

DEDICATED

TO

A. C. H.

H. W. S.

CONTENTS

INTRODUCTION

Buddhism as a separate religion has almost ceased to exist in India; yet it is part, and a vital part, of India's great heritage.

It has left its mark upon her great buildings, and not less upon her national consciousness. Not only did it absorb and crystallize much from the Hinduism out of which it sprang, and express much of Hindu aspirations and ideals, but it has in turn been reabsorbed into that amazing creed and has given of its life and spirit to it.

Especially is this true of the ethical teaching of Gautama Buddha. This is a heritage for which India can hardly be too grateful; for it has been her greatest weakness that she has never risen to the conception of a Righteous God, and so has missed the moral fibre which that conception alone can impart. And whilst Gautama himself failed of this sublime achievement, and therefore failed to hold her allegiance, yet he taught of a Force 'which makes for righteousness', and his own example of pure and loving manhood has been a mighty power for good.

Had India been able to seize the best in Buddhism, and to blend it with her mystic intuition of the reality and the nearness of God, how different her story would have been! And to-day when the Christ, purer, more loving, more majestic and mighty to save, is beginning in strange and incalculable ways to dominate her sub-consciousness, and to dictate the programme of her social reforms, it is being seen that Gautama, agnostic though he was, was yet a forerunner, and is still a prophetic voice of whom she has much to learn.

> 'Give me the strength', she cries, 'lightly to bear my joys and sorrows.
> Give me the strength to make my love fruitful in service.
> Give me the strength never to disown the poor, or bend my knees before insolent might.'[1]

Such strength is truly a 'gift', and it is not Gautama's to give; but sage advice, and winning example, and the incentive of a lofty ideal in which barriers of caste are broken down and men live peaceably together,—these are not valueless.

To the Eastern reader, therefore, I offer this little anthology, believing that it has its own place in the Heritage of India Series. And I trust that it may also find acceptance in the West, and may contribute something to the study of a religion which is exercising many minds, and is so often misunderstood alike by friend and foe.

The Western student of Buddhism is almost inevitably fascinated by what H. C. Warren has called 'the strangeness of the intellectual landscape'; yet he is not seldom bewildered and even alienated by the mass of its literature and by its numberless repetitions. Slowly the conviction dawns on him that he is in a kind of maze, that he has passed the same way many times, and is not, at the end of his wanderings, greatly advanced towards the heart of the religion.

That Buddhism, in spite of its critics, *is* a religion,

[1] From Rabindranath Tagore's *Gitanjali*, which more than any other book expresses the loftiest aspirations of the soul of modern India.

and that it has a heart, will be abundantly clear to the candid student; in fact, it may, in a sense, be said to wear its heart upon its sleeve! Certainly there is nothing esoteric, nothing of the closed hand in it, as so many writers of theosophic tendency would have us believe; and the Buddha himself protested that his message was a simple one:

> 'Even as the Ocean has everywhere but one taste—that of salt—so my doctrine has everywhere but one essence—that of deliverance.'
>
> 'One thing only do I teach: sorrow and the uprooting of sorrow.'

How wistfully have the hearts of his countrymen turned to these ideals;[1] and how significant it is that he threw open the way of salvation to all.[2] The heart of his religion may therefore be said to consist of a few great tenets of a practical kind which bear directly upon this 'one thing': the transiency of phenomena, which explains the sorrowfulness of things; the law of cause and effect, which brings home to the individual the reason for his own pain, and provides a solution of the problem of suffering; and, closely linked with this, the doctrine of transmigration in its Buddhistic guise, which amplifies this explanation and finds in expiation a meaning for the world.[3] So far Buddhism is inevitably metaphysical, though it rejects all speculation as to origins; and if it stopped here it would indeed deserve the charge of radical pessimism so often hurled at it. But its second step—'the uprooting of sorrow'—carries

[1] Cf. Nos. III, IV, XIV, XV, &c.
[2] Cf. Nos. XXXIX, XL.
[3] Cf. Nos. II–VII.

it out into the sphere of ethics, and here it strikes a note of sturdy optimism.

What is the cause of all the sorrow and pain of things? Does it lie outside man's control? No; the root of all evil lies in *Tanhā*, the will to be and to have; if we can but rid ourselves of this we shall be free indeed; and the way of freedom is the way of Buddhist righteousness.[1]

Broadly speaking, we may say there are two royal roads to emancipation—self-culture and altruism, or more exactly *meditation* and *benevolence*—and they lead to the attainment of that which amidst the flux and unreality of things is alone real and permanent.[2]

Such are the cardinal tenets of early Buddhism, and they have laid a strong hold upon the imagination and reason of Buddhists of every School, though often disfigured by modern accretions and primitive superstitions. Thus, widely as they differ in other respects, the Buddhism of Ceylon and Burma and the Buddhism of China, Japan, and Tibet are one in these fundamentals.

For the whole structure of Buddhism is reared upon that intuition of Gautama, which is known as his Enlightenment, and which he epitomized and gave to the world as the Four Aryan, or Noble, Truths; and being primarily a moral teacher he expounded very fully the ethical way of salvation. Just as Jesus in the Beatitudes showed men the conditions of entering the Kingdom of the Happy Life, analysing for them His own deep religious experience, so Gautama in his Eightfold Way sum-

[1] Cf. Nos. I, VII, VIII, IX, &c.

[2] Cf. Nos. XII, XIII, XXVIII, and XXXVI, XXXVII, XLV, &c.

marized his own experience in the long pursuit of happiness and peace. Both religions are to be regarded in one aspect as Paths to Happiness.[1]

Now the ethical as well as the metaphysical ideas of Buddhism may be found duly analysed and tabulated in scholastic lists and prosy dialogues, but they are far more attractively and not less accurately expressed in *gāthās*, or snatches of verse, scattered here and there through the sacred writings, or collected into such anthologies as the *Dhammapada*, *Sutta Nipāta* and *Theratherī-gāthā*, and these represent probably the most primitive strands of Buddhist lore.

In the conviction that the heart of a religion is best seen in its hymns, where there is more of spontaneity and usually less of dogma, I have translated some typical and popular Buddhist poems, and have ventured to call the collection 'The Heart of Buddhism'; for I believe that by careful study of these verses, the student will catch more of the spirit of Buddhism, and, what is more important, enter far more deeply into the feelings of Buddhists, than by much wading through the prose books.

Is it not true that we get nearer to the spirit of Christ and to the heart of Christian experience in such hymns as Newman's 'Lead, Kindly Light', and Matheson's 'O Love, that wilt not let me go', and in poems like Francis Thompson's 'Hound of Heaven', than in most volumes of theology or even of sermons? And in the songs and ejaculations of the Buddhist Elders we find the expression of a true and deep experience, from which we may learn

[1] Cf Nos. VIII, IX, &c.

much of the strange blending of joy and stoicism [1] and of benevolence and self-culture [2] which characterized Buddhism in its Golden Age.

Mrs. Rhys Davids, to whom the Buddhist world owes so much, has expressed in her admirable edition of the *Therī-gāthā* a doubt whether 'even the pious Buddhist believes that these verses contain the *ipsissima verba* of those members of the Order to whom they are ascribed, or that these notable adherents conversed in Pali *Slokas*'. Yet this is what almost all Buddhists *do* believe! In Ceylon I have lain awake at night listening to the driver of the bullock-wagon and his mate conversing in impromptu stanzas; and in the East, where memory is wonderfully retentive, it is not incredible that tradition should descend in this way. But whether the *gāthās* were quite spontaneous or not, we can feel that they are the naïve utterance in many cases of a real and true experience, and we can gather something of the magnetism and power of the personality who called forth such enthusiasm.

It is essential in studying Buddhism to get a true and sympathetic mental picture of the great Teacher himself. This is not easy; for many of the dialogues are scholastic inventions, stiff and wooden; and most of the statues are purely conventional. But the parable translated below, under the title 'The Teacher a Farmer',[3] gives us a very winsome and withal humorous portrait, and I have seen at any rate one statuette in which the sculptor seemed to have caught something of its spirit.

I had wandered into one of the picturesque

[1] Cf. Nos. XVII, XXIV, XXV, XXVII, XXXI, &c.
[2] Cf. Nos. XII, XXXVI, XLI, &c. [3] No. I.

vihāras of Ceylon with clean-swept courtyard and gleaming white *dāgoba* and venerable Bo-tree, all set in a bowery wilderness of palms and ferns and scented shrubs—an ‘abode of peace’ such as that described in No. XI. Here in this lovely casket were enshrined the usual massive images of the Buddha with his attendant disciples Moggallāna and Sāriputta, vast seated figures in deep meditation with eyes closed, or standing colossi, with eyes staring and inexpressive. Before them were placed countless smaller images in brass or silver, pathetic offerings of pilgrims; and not one of them departed from the conventional pattern, or showed any expression other than that of repose. As we came out, glad to escape from the stupefying atmosphere of the shrine, heavy with the scent of jasmine and ‘temple-flowers’ and camphor, we were greeted by a very old *bhikkhu*,[1] who asked us if we could do anything for his eyes, which were swollen and inflamed. We returned in a little while and treated them for him. Meanwhile he had been bringing out his treasures to show us, and a group of villagers and temple-boys and younger *bhikkhus* had gathered round. With trembling eager fingers, the old man unwrapped layer after layer of cloth and silk and showed us the most perfect image of the Buddha I have seen. It was about two feet high, of very old ivory, and carved, he told us, in the fifteenth century as a royal gift from the King of Ceylon to the King of Siam. The pose was the conventional one of the Buddha as Teacher: standing with hand held up, the thumb and forefinger together, as though he were expounding some nice point of doctrine.

[1] Buddhist monk.

But it was the face which at once riveted attention ; it was so kindly and so humorous, a smile playing about the corners of the mouth and an expression in the eyes such as Socrates must have worn as he quizzed his adolescent disciples.

Such was Sākyamuni, who loved to call himself a physician of the soul, and whose greatest joy was to open the eyes of men blinded with passion, or to stab the soul of the sluggard awake. The Four Noble Truths are, in fact, as Kern has pointed out, an adaptation of current Indian medical lore to the needs of the soul, and it was thus that the Teacher conceived his work. But gradually, within two or three centuries, myth and legend surrounded his story, and his humanity was hid under a heavy superstructure of miracle. Such is the Buddha as the modern unsophisticated Buddhist loves to think of him—an omniscient victor and, in a sense, a Saviour able to impart his merit to others.[1] And Northern Buddhism was only carrying this line of development further when it deified him, developing the doctrine of justifying faith in Amida, and making the Highest Bliss consist in entrance into his Paradise. But Southern Buddhism has on the whole continued to think of him as Teacher and has treasured summaries of his teachings. Familiar examples are the Mahāmangala Sutta[2] and the Vyaggapajja Sutta,[3] which are known to almost all cultured Buddhists and give in concise and attractive form the whole duty of the layman.

The doctrines of Karma and of Transmigration have become deeply embedded in the Buddhist

[1] Cf. No. XLII. [2] No. IX. [3] No LIII.

consciousness, of which indeed they form the very warp and woof. No one who has not lived in India can realize how great and subtle is the hold which these doctrines have laid upon the imagination and reason of even the simple villager. And here it is well to note that whilst Gautama strove to refine upon the Brahminical doctrine of Transmigration and to substitute, for a transmigrating soul, passing, as in the Upanishads, like a caterpillar from leaf to leaf, a stream of energy clothing itself in body after body, yet modern Buddhists for the most part revert to the older philosophy; and I have therefore not included any passages which deal with the differences between the two doctrines; they may be best studied in that very attractive work the *Milinda Pañha*, or 'Questions of King Menander'. I have also omitted passages dealing with the nature of Nirvāna, for it is possible to support any of the current theories concerning it from the Sacred Books, and Buddhists for the most part are not troubling themselves about it, but look forward rather to rebirth in a heaven or upon earth under favourable conditions.

There are certain other controverted subjects, however, which are of more practical import and which are always recurring, and I hope some light will be found upon them in these pages. The so-called 'pessimism' of the Buddha may, for instance, be studied by setting side by side Nos. XIX and XX, in which a pessimistic attitude towards the *Body* is revealed, with Nos. XXIV and XXV, which show a sturdy optimism towards the *Mind* of man. Again, the still vexed question of the place of love in Buddhism may be studied by contrasting No. XXXVI, which inculcates benevolence to all, with Nos. XLVIII and XLIX, which teach attachment to none. And some material for an estimate of the Buddha's attitude to women, another controversial question, may be gathered from Nos. XXX, XXXII and XXXIII.

The stories included are rather specimens than an adequate selection; they are included as throwing further light upon the topics of the poems; and all are popular with modern Buddhists. A knowledge of them as of the poems is of great importance to the Missionary and the Civil Servant, and indeed to any one whose lot is cast in Buddhist lands and who is not too insular to desire the friendship of the people of these lands.

Every student of the subject will probably have his own idea of what should and what should not be included in a collection making so bold a claim: some may, for instance, object to the supernatural element, which is rather largely represented; to the presence of stories of ogresses, or of charms for snakes, or of the plea for departed spirits. My own feeling is that I have not included enough of such matter, for it undoubtedly plays a very significant part in the Buddhism of to-day: the 'Pirit' ceremonies are very common both in Ceylon and Burma[1]; and the poems used on these occasions are very well known. Others may object that too large a place is given to the Sangha, or celibate Order of Monks, and to the importance of gifts made to them; but though the 'yellow-robed brethren' are too often corrupt, they wield an enormous power, and modern Buddhism is in a large measure

[1] Cf. No. XLII, IV, note.

a doctrine of merit obtained by gifts to the *bhikkhus*. For millions of modern Buddhists, Buddhism is almost equivalent to this doctrine of merit so obtained, a doctrine which is killing its very soul. I do not expect to escape criticism, but I humbly offer these renderings as an honest attempt to reproduce the spirit of the originals, and they are for the most part literal translations.

I have to express my gratitude to my friends Pundit W. D. C. Wagiswara, of the Government Training School, Colombo, and Samana Punnananda, of Calcutta University, for help in locating certain passages and in translating certain others. Mr. Wagiswara and I translated the *Thera-gāthā* together some two years ago from a palm-leaf manuscript belonging to one of the Kandy temples; and it has been a pleasant recreation which has helped to while away the tedium of a sea-voyage and a convalescence to put our rendering of them and some other translations into verse.

To the Rev. G. K. A. Bell I owe some valuable suggestions.

I must express my thanks also to Mr. D. J. Subasinha of Ceylon for permission to include two of his translations (Nos. XLIX and LIII), and to Prof. Charles Duroiselle of the Burma Archaeological Survey and to Prof. Rhys Davids for similar permission to reprint Nos. XLIV and XLVII respectively.

Lastly, I am glad to thank my Mother, who transcribed the whole text for me, when I was too ill or too lazy to do it myself. She tells me she has learnt to honour the memory of the Buddha, and if others are led to do so by this little book I shall be glad. Still more do I hope that it will prove useful to those who are striving to lead the followers of the great dead Teacher to Him who is Life indeed, and who blends in His Sacred Person the Righteousness of Gautama's ideal with the Mystic Passion of the heart of India.

RANGOON, *December* 5, 1913.

I

THE TEACHER A FARMER

(Sutta Nipāta, Uravagga.)

THUS have I heard:

The Blessed One was dwelling in Māgadha at Dukkhināgiri in the Brahman village Ekanāla, where the Brahman Kasibhāvadraga had five hundred ploughs at work; for it was the time of ploughing. One morning the Blessed One, taking robe and bowl, came to the field where they were working. Now it was the time for breaking the fast, and he, awaiting his turn, stood on one side.

The Brahman saw him standing there, and thus accosted him: 'I, O recluse, plough and sow, and then only do I eat. So should'st thou, O recluse, plough and sow and thereafter eat!'

'I also, O Brahman, plough and sow,' said he, 'nor do I eat till I have ploughed and sown.'

'Nay, but I see no yoke nor plough, no ploughshare nor goad, no beasts of burden belonging to the Reverend Gautama.'

Then up spake the Blessed One again:

'I also, O Brahman, plough and sow, and having ploughed and sown, I eat.'

To whom the Brahman made answer in these verses:

'O Gautama, if farmer thou
As thou so brazenly declarest,
Where are thine oxen and thy plough?
Come, idle braggart, show us how
The field for harvest thou preparest!'

To him the Blessed One made answer:

'A Farmer I, good sir, indeed.
Right Views my very fruitful seed;
The rain that waters it is Discipline.
Wisdom herself my yoke and plough.
(Brahman, do'st take my meaning, now?)
The pole is maiden Modesty,
And Mindfulness the axle-tree;
Alertness is my goad and ploughshare keen!

Guarded in thought and act and speech
With Truthfulness I weed the ground;
In gentle Kindliness is found
The Way of Salvation I preach.
My ox is Endeavour,
Which beareth me ever,
Where Grief cometh never,
To Nirvāna, the Goal I shall reach.

Such, good Brahman, is my farming,
And it bears ambrosial crops:
Whoso follows out my Teaching
Straight for him all sorrow stops.'

Then the Brahman Kasibhāvadraga poured rice-milk into a golden bowl and offered it to the Blessed One, saying:

'A Farmer thou in very sooth,
Ambrosial is thy crop of Truth!
Drink the rice-milk, sir, I pray thee;
Gladly do I now obey thee!'

The story goes on to relate that the Buddha took the rice-milk, and pouring it into water, caused it to hiss and splutter. On seeing this marvel the

Brahman was fully converted and admitted to the Sangha, afterwards becoming an Arahat.

NOTE

The same story occurs also in Samyutta Nikāya, VII. 2. 1.

II

VANITAS, OMNIA VANITAS

(Visuddhi Magga XVII.)

ALL ye who live in sensual joy
And take delight in carnal lust,
Shall feel, when sensuous pleasures cloy
Grief's smarting, piercing arrow-thrust.

III

DISILLUSION

(Theragāthā, 72.)

SICKNESS and palsied tottering Eld,
Yea, Death itself these eyes beheld!
From such dread sights to free my mind
I left what most I loved behind.

NOTE

The experience of this *bhikkhu* seems to have followed that of the Buddha himself, who, obsessed with the sight of a leper, an old man and a corpse, left all to find a way of escape from suffering.

IV

THE MISERY OF LIFE

(From the Introduction to the Jātaka Book.)

As some poor sufferer in prison pent
  From year to weary year is racked by pain,
Longs for release and cannot find content,
  But ever pines and chafes against his chain
So do thou see in each succeeding birth
  A prison full of untold misery!
Seek to shake off all chains that bind to earth
  And from existence evermore be free.

NOTE

Nos. XLV–XLVII are specimens of the 550 'Birth-stories' which comprise the Jātaka Book.

V

KARMA

(Vasettha Sutta.)

ACTION the whole wide world is fashioning,
By action man is ever being made:
'Tis action fetters every living thing,
As the whole chariot by its pole is swayed

NOTE

By acting, a man creates fresh Karma, the effects of which must work themselves out. Thus the course of the world and the lives and destinies of individuals are being from moment to moment determined. The almost inevitable deduction from this teaching is that *inaction* offers a way of freedom from these fetters, and Eastern monachism tends always to this solution.

The doctrine is well summed up in the Milinda Pañha in words attributed to Gautama:

'Each being has his own action: each is heir to his own action: each is the fruit of his own action's womb: each is kinsman of his own action, and each has his own action as over-lord and protector. It is their own actions that divide men up, allotting them to high or low estate.'

The Sage Nāgasena quotes the above as throwing light upon the inequality of human destinies.

VI

KARMA

(Anguttara Nikāya III. 33.[1])

THE harvest of thy former birth
Must now be reaped upon this Earth
For be they many, be they few,
(O Monks, the Law is known to you
Deeds done in envy or in hate,
Deeds of the fool infatuate,
Must bear their fitting punishment,
Till Karma's energy be spent
For lustful thought and angry word
No entry to thy life afford,
But recognize thy proper doom
And yield just retribution room:
Who seeketh wisdom flings the gate
Wide open to his fitting fate!

NOTE

To see things as they are, and to accept the inevitable with a stoic fortitude—this is true wisdom according to the Buddha.

VII

FOUR SORROWFUL THINGS: A RIDDLE AND AN ANSWER

(Samyutta Nikāya 1.[6])

'What bringeth human life to Earth?
What still disdaineth to be bound?
Who pass in woe from birth to birth?
From what can no release be found?'

''Tis Passion bringeth man to earth,
His mind disdaineth to be bound,
All sentient beings know rebirth,
From misery no escape is found!'

VIII

ANOTHER RIDDLE AND ITS ANSWER

(Sutta Nipāta 1.[10])

These are some of the questions put to Gautama by the demon Alāvaka, who threatened if he could not answer them to hurl him into the Ganges. (See below, No. XLII.)

The demon speaks:

'What is the best that men possess?
What brings them truest happiness?
What is the sweetest of the sweet?
What is the life of lives most meet?'

Gautama answers:

'Faith is the best that men possess,
The Law brings truest happiness,
Truth is the sweetest of the sweet,
The life of Insight is most meet!'

IX

THE SONG OF GREAT BLESSING

(Mahāmangala Sutta : Sutta Nipāta II.[4])

This famous poem—an epitome of Buddhist ethics—is known to almost all Buddhists of any culture; and in Burma every child, however humble, learns it, the *Mingala Thot* being one of his first lessons. In Ceylon and other Buddhist lands it is being increasingly taught.

In the stress it lays upon the so-called 'passive' virtues, humility, patience, reverence, purity, contentment, it reminds us of the Sermon on the Mount. It may, in fact, be regarded as a kind of Buddhist Beatitudes, depicting the Happy Life as the Buddha conceived it.

In the original each couplet contains the words, 'This is the greatest blessing, or happiness.'

Thus have I heard:

Once when the Blessed One was at Jetavana in Anathapindika's Park, as night came on, a beautiful *deva* (god) drew near, lighting up the whole place with his presence. He greeted the Blessed One, and then standing on one side, addressed him in these verses:

'What countless men and deities,
Desiring Bliss, have sought to find—
Come tell me, Master,* what it is
That brings most blessing to mankind.'

* This is eloquent of the position of the gods in Buddhism: they are still in the thrall of Karma, and therefore inferior to the good Buddhist. Here the god appears as a learner; but see XLII, Jayamangala Gāthā, Stanza V, note.

To whom the sage made answer :

'To shun the fool, to court the wise,
This is the highest Paradise :

Pay ye respect where it is due,
So will true blessing wait on you :

Seek a fit place and there remain,
Striving self-knowledge to attain :

If in past lives you've stored up merit,
The fruits thereof you'll now inherit :

Let wisdom, skill, and discipline,
And gracious kindly words be thine :

Tend parents, cherish wife and child,
Pursue a blameless life and mild :

Live thou devout, give ample alms,
Protect thy kin from life's alarms.

Do good, shun ill, and still beware
Of the red wine's insidious snare :

So do thou persevere in good :
This is the true Beatitude :

Be humble, with thy lot content,
Grateful and ever reverent :

Study the Law of Righteousness,
This is the path that leads to Bliss

Be patient thou, the Saints frequent
And ponder still their argument :

The Noble Truths, the life austere
And chaste that brings Nirvāna here :[1]

The life from eightfold bond secure,[2]
The life of peace that crowns the pure :

This is the Highest Bliss to find,
This the chief blessing of mankind.

NOTES

[1] *Nirvāna in this world* is the calm and serene state of mind of the Arahat, wholly detached from the things of time and space.

[2] *From eightfold bond.* The eight attachments are : Sorrow and joy, fame and contumely, wealth and poverty, gain and loss. If a man is moved by none of these things, he is a happy man.

Another very popular summary of Buddhist ethics is found in the Dhammapada 183 :

Eschew all sin ;
Good deeds begin ;
Cleanse every thought ;
Thus Buddhas taught.

X

THE TRUE RECLUSES: A DIALOGUE

(Therīgāthā, 271–90.)

This is perhaps the most artistic of the charming *Psalms of the Sisters*, inasmuch as it contains something of dramatic development and a good deal of quiet humour. Rohinī gives the purest motives for her love of the yellow-robed brotherhood: the worldly-minded householder adds the motive of self-interest; and she quietly brings him back to the realities—this time with good effect!

As a contemporary picture of the early Sangha, this poem is of unique interest.

' "See, Father, see the holy men," thou criest,
Awaking me from sleep, O Rohinī:
And ever art thou praising the recluses!
Say, daughter, would'st thou join their company?
Forever dost thou feed them on my substance:
Say why are these recluses dear to thee?

A lazy crew of idle good-for-nothings,
Who batten on the food of honest men!
Cadgers they are, and fond of dainty feeding;
Why dost thou love them, daughter, tell me then?'

'Full many a time, O Father, hast thou asked me!
Come now I'll tell thee of their lofty work;
For workers truly are they of the noblest;
Battle with hate and lust they do not shirk.

Must I not love them? For their work is holy,
Holy in inward thought and word and deed,
As pearl or ocean-shell so pure and lustrous,
Untainted they by hatred, sloth, or greed.

Versed in the Righteous Law they are, and skilful :
Aye, and they practise too the law they preach ;
Learnèd and self-possessed and ever watchful,
Living in all things as the Sages teach.

Must I not love them ? Far afield they wander,
Wise and so lowly-minded and discreet ;
Knowing the end of every ill and sorrow—
See, Father, how they pace the village street !

Downcast their eyes ; their paces measured, sober,
They meditate, nor look to left or right :
They lay not up on earth the fleeting treasure ;
Finished their quest, their lofty goal in sight !

Poor are they too, yet touch not gold nor silver ;
Each day supplies for them their simple needs ;
From many lands and towns they join the Order,
Bound in the sacred tie of loving deeds.'

'Lucky the day when thou wast born, O maiden !
Firm-founded is thy faith in Jewels Three.
These are the harvest-fields, as well thou knowest,
Where there is very fruitful husbandry.
I too will serve the worthy true recluses ;
Such service is repaid most bounteously ! '

'Father, if any evil apprehending
Thou would'st be wholly rid of evil's snare,
Go get thee to the Master and take refuge,
Straight to the Holy Norm do thou repair ;
Aye, and whate'er the noble Bhikkhus bid thee
That do : for truest happiness lies there.'

'Lo, now I'll hie me straightway to the Buddha,
His holy teaching from the Bhikkhus I'll obtain:
So shall I too observe the noble precepts
And the best bliss on earth I'll surely gain.'

(*Later.*)

'Erst was I but by noble birth a Brahman,
This day am I a Brahman made in sooth,
Attaining to the threefold Vedic Knowledge,
Bathed in the cleansing waters of the Truth.' [1]

NOTE

[1] The reference is to cleansing ablutions performed by the Brahman student before leaving his teacher's house, after acquiring knowledge of the Three Vedas.

The Buddha adapted the term *tevijjo,* and made it mean 'versed in the three attainments of the Arahat'—knowledge of former births, the eye of insight, and the purging out of all taints of impurity.

XI

THE ABODE OF PEACE

(Chulla Vagga VI.[1])

These stanzas are attributed to Gautama Buddha, and give thanks for a gift of sixty monastic cells made by a lay-adherent to the Sangha. Caves of this kind still exist, notably at Nasik and Karli, looking out over wide and peaceful vistas and forming ideal spots for meditation and undisturbed quiet.

It is very moving to stand in one of these ancient monasteries and to reflect that here for many centuries the peaceful ' Sons of the Buddha ' led the ' strenuous life of meditation ', centuries before that great tableland had become the battlefield of the Marathas and the Moghuls.

HERE cold and heat no sojourn make,
Here ravenous beasts no entry find,
Nor stinging fly, nor creeping snake,
Winter's cold rain nor summer's scorching wind.

Here is a place to concentrate
The thoughts, to dwell serene, apart,
Where men of insight meditate—
Such habitations charm the Sage's heart !

These are choice gifts : therefore ye wise,
Having your own best weal in mind,
Let sacred edifices rise
To lodge the holy Brethren of mankind

Raiment and fitting drink and food
And ample bedding now prepare!
These offer to the Brotherhood;
Let them in turn the Righteous Law declare.

So shall your misery remove,
And ye be purged of every stain,
Goodness and Truth ye'll learn to love,
And loving shall the longed-for Goal attain!

Note

In this poem the following points in Buddhist ethics are noteworthy:

1. *The division of labour:* The Sangha to meditate, the laymen to provide. (Compare S. Paul, Romans xv. [27], 1 Cor. ix. [11].)
2. The Teacher appeals frankly *to the motive of self-advancement:* Buddhist ethics are ultimately hedonistic.
3. *There is much merit in giving gifts to the Sangha:* The India of Aśoka was thickly sown with such 'sacred edifices', and Behar gets its name from the number of 'Vihāras' it contained. In the Burma of to-day pagodas form a distinctive part of the landscape, and at Pagān there are said to be a thousand. Where we say 'as many as the stars' the Burman says 'as many as the pagodas of Pagān'. It is I think, true to say that Buddhism is tending more and more to emphasize this doctrine of 'Merit' and Christianity to reject it.

XII

MEDITATION

(Theragāthā, 307.)

(Selected.)

WHITE against the dark storm-cloud
Homeward fly the frightened cranes ;
The cave they seek is hid by rains ;
The toads awakened croak aloud :
Here where the streamlets rush in spate
Beneath dark trees I'll meditate.

(Ibid., 211.)

BIG with rain is the stormy sky ;
The crested peacock calls his mate ;
The earth gleams fresh with greenery ;
A fitting time to meditate.

In Buddha's precepts be not slack !
Hard to travel is the track
That leads to Bliss : no turning back !

NOTE

These poems, like many in the 'Songs of the Brethren', show a strong appreciation of natural scenery as an aid to the 'religious' life.

XIII

HEROIC MEASURES

(Ibid., 193.)

NOT for sleep is the star-spangled night
But for work and vigil, O Sage!
What if the elephant's rider unseated
Be mauled by the brute in his rage? *
Better for me, than to live on defeated,
Is to die in the thick of the fight!

XIV

HOLDING THE MIRROR UP TO NATURE

(Ibid., 169.)

THE barber came to dress my hair:
I took the mirror from his hand,
And in it all my body scanned:
And whilst I gazed, lo! then and there
I knew the vileness of the flesh:
So broke I through the clinging mesh
Of Ignorance, and cast aside
The unclean garment of my pride.
Now stript of Vanity I go;
No more shall I be born to woe!

* As the elephant is a dangerous but very useful mount, so meditation, even though it prove too strenuous a practice, is the way to peace.

XV

A CONVERTED WORLDLING

(Ibid., 157.)

A WORLDLING I who gave my mind to dress,
A thrall to pride and wanton wickedness,
Until I listened to the Sage,
And let his gracious words assuage
My craving thirst for sensuous happiness.

XVI

NOBLESSE OBLIGE

(Ibid., 173.)

As when a blood horse falls beneath the shafts
And, stung with shame, doth struggle to arise,
So think of me, a nobly-gendered son
Whom the great Teacher's insight maketh wise.

XVII

A HERO OF THE SOLITARY WAY

(Ibid., 95.)

BLIND and alone my way I wend,
The desert sands before, behind :
Shunning the haunts of evil men,
Here let me die, alone and blind !

XVIII

ALL IS FLEETING

(Ibid., 145.)

Days and nights go speeding past;
  Life itself doth pass away;
As the river rushing fast,
  Men hasten by, and may not stay!
Though they would its sting ignore,
Fools the doom of sin endure:
Retribution cometh sure!

XIX

A MEMENTO MORI*

(Ibid., 151.)

See Kālī trussed for burial, loathsome sight!
Clumsy and huge she lies, the crow-black trull:
Broken her limbs, and from her broken skull
The clotted brain like curd comes oozing white.
Such, such is mortal woman! Ponder thou
  The ghastly wreckage of mortality;
For loving such men are reborn, I trow,
  From misery to endless misery!

* My excuse for including this very horrible poem is that this practice of gazing at dead bodies and skeletons till disgust arises and detachment from the world follows, is still in use in Buddhist lands. There are other Buddhist poems much more offensive than this.

XX

THE BODY

(Milinda Pañha, 73.[24])

THIS body is a nest of loathly sores;
A dank and slippery skin doth wrap it round;
And from a thousand thousand oozing pores
It sendeth out its stenches, like an open wound.

NOTE

'Buddhism is the religion of analysis.'

The Buddha, whose central thought is that all is transient and fleeting, sought to stab men's minds awake by many such a 'Memento Mori' as the above. If they would only analyse the body into its constituent parts and see it as it is, they would cease to love it and to pamper it, and desire would die out in them.

The following passage, which is not without a certain grim humour, emphasizes the same point; to the mind which is truly detached 'beauty is but skin deep'.

XXI

'THE VIEW DEPENDS UPON THE POINT OF VIEW'

(A paraphrase. Visuddhi Magga, I.)

THE Elder Mahatissa was meditating near Anuradhapura one early morning, when a beautiful and richly-dressed woman passed him and laughed back at him, seeking to captivate. Seeing her flashing teeth, he was reminded that the body is a set of bones, and impure.

The Elder saw her teeth agleam,
And straight disgust surged up within:
'How foul this body, rightly seen!
So think, and ye to Truth shall win.'

Soon her husband in pursuit came up with the Elder and asked, 'Did you, O reverend sir, see a woman pass this way?' To whom he made answer:

'Or man or woman passed me now,
Good sir, I cannot rightly say:
But this at least is sure, I trow,
A skeleton hath gone this way!'

NOTE

A mediaeval Western carving in ivory, now in the Fitzwilliam Museum at Cambridge, represents in front a beautiful woman, behind a skull.

XXII

THE HOG

(Theragāthā, 17.)

LIKE a hog to the trough
Goes the fool to the womb!
Everlasting rebirth
Is the sluggard's sure doom.

NOTE

The hog in Buddhism stands for sloth—one of its three cardinal vices.

XXIII

PERSEVERANCE

(Ibid., 246.)

1. *Crede experto.*

ONCE hadst thou Faith, now hast it not ?
  That is *thy* fault, not mine, O Son.
Frail is this wavering faith, I wot :
  Men grasp, lose hold, and are undone !
But these old legs are strong and stout :
  To beg my food I must set out :
A little there, a little here !
  Thus do thou also persevere.

2. *Hope for the Climber.*

(Ibid., 62.)

HE who falls may rise again :
Falling lose not heart of hope !
Up the steep and slippery slope
I too struggled to attain :
And, because I loved the good,
Swift I found Beatitude !

XXIV

THE VICTORY OF THE STOIC

(Ibid., 39.)

DISEASE assailed this mortal frame,
And straight my mind awoke :
' Come, play the man ! ' within me spoke
A voice that to the rescue came.

NOTE

This little poem admirably contrasts the transient frail *body* with the eternal *mind* of man. Similarly the following poem contrasts the body, in its dull commonplace surroundings, with the 'far-wandering' mind, which may not be bound.

XXV

THE KINGDOM OF THE MIND

(Ibid., 14.)

BLEST is the lesson my teacher has taught !
I live in the village, but ever in thought
I escape to the jungle : no fetters for me,
For wisdom hath set me most gloriously free !

XXVI

THE UNDAUNTED HEART

(Ibid., 189.)

ALONE dwell I in dreadful cave,
The rain pours gurgling ceaselessly :
These things for me no terrors have ;
Heeding them not, my mind is free.

XXVII

A CONTENTED MIND IS A BLESSING KIND

(Ibid., 207.)

COLD and dark is the winter's night ;
  It chaps the skin ; it freezes thought !
Where shall the shivering bhikkhu lie ?
  Into safe barns the harvest 's brought ;
The Māgadhans rejoice ; and I
  Rejoice with them : I'll sleep all right
  In good warm straw this winter's night !

NOTE

The people of Magadha were fellow countrymen of Gautama Buddha.

XXVIII

THE STRENUOUS LIFE OF MEDITATION

(Ibid., 231.)

' Too cold for work, too hot, too late it is ! '
Men think and lose their opportunities.
    But some of heat and cold make light
    And work away in their despite :
Come seek we jungle-solitude
And cultivate the strenuous mood !

XXIX

A BUDDHIST S. ANTHONY

(Ibid., 267.)

FRAGRANT with sandal-wood and garlanded,
  A girl was dancing gaily in the street
With softest strains of flute accompanied.
  I chanced upon my begging round to meet
The harlot, as she plied her shameful trade:
  'O Snare by Māra set, licentious jade'—
    My gorge arose—my mind was free!
    The Dharma's work behold in me,
    Fruit of the Sage's husbandry!

NOTE

This poem provides an instructive contrast between Christian and Buddhist ethics. An Egyptian hermit of the Early Christian Church also met a dancing-girl plying her shameful trade. He burst into tears, exclaiming, 'Alas! that she should be at such pains to please men in her sinful vocation: whilst we in our holy calling use so little diligence to please God.'

The Buddhist saint is disgusted, but rejoices that he himself is not tempted. The Christian saint weeps that the children of this world are more zealous than the children of light.

XXX

MARRIED LOVE IS LUST

(Ibid., 299.)

WITH handmaidens and jewels rare
Of womankind surpassing fair,
  Our little boy upon her arm,
    My wife came, seeking me.

But I, of evil lures aware,
Beheld in her a subtle snare,
Designed to do me deadly harm,
Disguised by Māra's treachery!
Such bonds have lost their hold on me,
They chain him not whose mind is free.

XXXI

A NEW MAN

(Ibid., 43.)

Happy I in freedom blithe!
Three crooked things I've laid aside:
The plough, the hoe, the heavy scythe:
There they lie: there let them bide!
The strenuous life of meditation free,
This is the life henceforth for me!

XXXII

A NEW WOMAN

(Therīgāthā, 11.)

Happy freedom! Liberated bride!
To bondage never to return!
Three crooked things are laid aside
My mortar, and my butter-churn;
Aye, and my crooked hunchback lord:
Freedom from birth and death 's assured

XXXIII

UNSAFE CONFIDANTS

(Milinda Pañha, IV.[16])

NINE beings are unstable, fickle, mean:
The lustful, angry, easily beguiled,
The coward, too, and he who seeks for gain,
Women and eunuchs, the drunkard and the child:
For what is told to them in secrecy
The public comes to know immediately!

NOTE

This poem is chiefly of interest as helping us to realize Gautama's view of women. That this low estimate of women was really his seems clear from two other passages:

1. Anguttara Nikāya, IV.[8]:

> 'Why is it, Reverend One, that women never sit in public assemblies, nor do business, nor go to far countries on public affairs?'
>
> 'Women, O Ānanda, are irritable, and envious, miserly and foolish. For these reasons they do not sit in public assemblies, nor do business, nor go on embassies.'

2. Chulla Vagga, X.[16]:

> 'As when a blight of mildew falls on the ripe crop of rice, O Ānanda, that crop is doomed: so in whatever religion and doctrine women are allowed to leave home for the homeless state, that religion will come to a speedy end.'

XXXIV

A FATHER GREETS HIS SON

FINDING HIM IN THE COMPANY OF THE BUDDHA

(Theragāthā, 177.)

As lions roaring each to each in mountain cave,
So speak we, heroes who have wisely fought and won,
Defeating Māra and his host of warriors brave :
Victorious father greeteth thus victorious son;
'Gladsome the sight to a father's old eyes,
Beholding his son in the ranks of the wise !
We have honoured the Teacher, respected the Law,
And reverenced the Sangha. Rejoice evermore!'

XXXV

A SON GREETS HIS MOTHER

WHO IS WEEPING BECAUSE HE HAS TAKEN THE YELLOW ROBE

(Ibid., 44.)

A MOTHER may mourn for her dear dead son,
Yea, she may mourn for her absent one :
But why lament, Lady Mother, for me
Whom here in the flesh thou now dost see !

XXXVI

COMPASSION

(Sutta Nipāta, 148–9.)

As, recking nought of self, a mother's love
Enfolds and cherishes her only son,
So through the world let thy compassion move
And compass living creatures every one,
Soaring and sinking in unfettered liberty,
Free from ill-will, purged of all enmity!

Note

Buddhaghośa, the great commentator of the fourth century A. D., commenting upon this passage, gives a beautiful analysis of a mother's love for her son:

Her yearning over the infant is *Mettā*, benevolence: her longing for his recovery from sickness is *Karunā*, pity: her joy at his growing powers is *Muditā*, sympathy: and her attitude of detachment when he is married and has a home of his own is *Upekhā*, non-interference.

A very fair idea of what Buddhism means by love may be gathered from this passage and from Nos. XLVIII and XLIX.

XXXVII

COMPASSION TO ANIMALS

A CHARM AGAINST SNAKES

This 'charm,' which reminds us of the Fairies' Song in *Midsummer Night's Dream,* may well be a bit of pre-Buddhistic folk-lore incorporated into the Buddhist books.*

It is related that a certain priest having been killed by snake-bite, the Buddha taught that it must have been the fault of the dead man for not exercising compassionate thoughts towards 'our little brothers' the snakes.

He then enjoined upon them the duty of cultivating such thoughts, and taught them a song to sing for their protection. It begins with a profession of love for the four 'royal families' of snakes and ends thus:

On things that crawl my love is shed,
On biped and on quadruped,
On those with many feet!
May crawling things do me no wrong,
May those that run on feet along
Do no offence to me!
All creatures that have life within,
And all our sentient kith and kin,
May ye from every hurt be free
And live beside us peacefully!

* Cf. the Atharva Veda.

Note

'Not killing' is the chief, often the only topic, of Buddhist preaching; and frescoes on the Temple walls warn Buddhists of the punishment that will follow in the next world. It is usually regarded in Buddhist lands as more heinous to kill a flea than to tell a lie.

XXXVIII

THE SPIRITS OF THE DEPARTED

(Tiro Khuddasuttam in Khuddaka Nikāya.)

The East will take more seriously than the West has done the beautiful doctrine of the Communion of Saints. In all Buddhist lands spirits play a vital part in the religion of the people. In Tibet Buddhism is almost entirely superseded by spirit-worship; in Burma the *Nats* are more thought of than the Buddhas; and in Japan and Ceylon any tree or deserted temple, any house or garden, may have its guardian deity.

This is readily understood if we reflect that every good man may become a god, and every bad man a demon; and the world is largely the stage upon which these spirit-armies wage their warfare. Thus every family will have its household god, who is some departed ancestor; and many a house has some snake or rat which is fed nightly—very much as Puck and the goblins were fed in Shakespeare's England by the unsophisticated. In many Buddhist lands there are regular occasions for 'feeding' the spirits of the departed.

According to a Japanese writer, the dead influence not only men's thoughts and actions, but also the conditions of nature: 'they direct the changes of the seasons, the wind and the rain, the good and the bad fortunes of states and of individual men.' And Gautama is recorded as having taught, as he lay dying, that there was 'not a spot for twelve leagues round of the size of the tip of a hair that was not crowded with powerful spirits'.

Of ancestor-worship in Japan, Lafcadio Hearn writes: 'It is probably the most profound and powerful of the emotions of the race—that which especially directs national life and shapes national character. Patriotism belongs to it. Filial piety depends upon it. Family love is rooted in it. Loyalty is based upon it.'

To the dim margin of the world of men,
Or to the cross-roads hungry spirits come,
Or by the junction of the walls they stand
Or at the threshold of their ancient home

And though there 's ample food and drink set out,
None thinks of them in thrall of iron fate,
Save here and there, some kindlier mindful soul
Looks to his kinsfolk's weal, compassionate ;

'Let this my honoured kinsmen's need supply,
And this their longing spirit-hearts rejoice' :
And they assent, and take the proffered food,
And bless him, uttering in a weak thin voice :

'Long live our kinsman, by whose kindly act
We now enjoy this rich and bounteous meal ;
For we his kith and kin are honourèd :
Now may this offering bring our kinsman weal.'

For there 's no farming in the spirit-world,
No tilth, nor herds, nor any merchandise :
Alms of the faithful are their only hope,
Their charity alone the under-world supplies.

For even as water droppeth from a crag,
And streams descending reach the far-off sea,
So do the gifts the faithful offer here
Pass to the spirit-world assuredly.

Then all their kindly deeds of former days,
The gifts they gave, the words of love they spoke,
Let us their kinsmen now recall to mind ;
They are our trusty friends, our own dear folk.

What boots for them your wailing and your tears ?
Mourning ye do but plough the desert sand !
But gifts made to the Sangha sure will bring
Rich harvests to the hungry wakeful spirit-band.

So doing shall ye purchase threefold merit,
Fulfilling duty to the needy dead;
For by your offerings to the pious Bhikkhus
Both they and ye are richly profited.

Note

All roads lead to Rome! So the Buddhist is led by many devious paths always back to this cardinal tenet—the supreme fruitfulness of offerings to the Sangha. It has become an obsession in modern Buddhism, and is sapping the vigour of Buddhist countries. There are as many as ten thousand Buddhist 'lamas', or priests, in Lhassa, and one-third of the arable land of Ceylon belongs to the monasteries. This teaching, which is still current among the Brahmans, that gifts to them will benefit the departed, seems to have passed over from Hinduism, in common with much else, to the Buddhists; and as young India is rebellious against the tyranny of the Brahman, so young Burma and Ceylon are beginning to see in the Sangha a 'Yellow Peril'! But this reaction is found only amongst the educated; the authority of Bhikkhus and Brahmans is still almost undisputed by the great bulk of the people.

XXXIX

THE TRUE BRAHMAN

(Dhammapada, 393–4.)*

Like other social reformers, Gautama set himself to redefine current terms. Very much as S. Paul redefined the term 'Jew', he gave to the proud title Brahman a new meaning, and showed that he is the true noble who acts nobly.

NOT matted hair nor heritage of birth
Can prove the Brahman ; nay, but sterling worth
And truthfulness and inward purity.
What boots your sackcloth and your tousled hair ?
On outward things, poor fools, ye lavish care !
Ye who are rotting, rotting, inwardly !

XL

LABELS, FALSE AND TRUE

(Vāsala Sutta.)

NOT by birth the Outcaste label,
Not by birth the Brahman know !
By actions only are we able
To judge a man or high or low.

* I have introduced into this anthology very little from the Dhammapada, because I have already published a translation of it under the title *The Buddha's Way of Virtue* in the 'Wisdom of the East' Series.

XLI

THE FALSE AND THE TRUE

(Ibid., 283.)

Borne on the flood of false austerity,
Full threescore years lived I, in misery!
Clothed me with dirt, and plucked out beard and
hair,
Fed me with dung, and sitting did forswear;
Refusing proffered hospitality,
I practised penances which lead to hell,*
Until I came beneath the Buddha's spell.
Behold the Dharma's glorious work in me;
Behold the Threefold Lore hath set me free!

Note

* '*Penances which lead to hell.*' Buddhism teaches that from false asceticism arise pride, ignorance, and false beliefs. It claims to be a Middle Path between the sensual life on the one hand and the ascetic life on the other.

XLII

THE SONG OF VICTORY AND BLESSING

(Jaya-mangala Gāthā.)

This mediaeval poem, probably composed in Siam, is very popular in Buddhist lands. It commemorates eight 'victories', some purely legendary, some founded upon fact, and is used as a kind of *mantra* or charm, the repetition of which is potent for good.

To the educated Buddhist, however, it is more in the nature of a meditation upon the Teacher—a reminder of his character and of his victorious example. From it we may learn much of the 'perfections' which make up the Buddhist Ideal.

I

By wondrous liberality
The Sage attained to victory,
Such was his chosen armoury!
Māra, by all his host attended,
With thousand flashing swords defended,
On his war-elephant so proudly seated,
In panoply of steel, the Sage defeated.
Be yours his glorious victory,
And yours its ample blessing be!

This stanza refers to the legendary attempts by Māra, King of Death and Lord of Hell, to prevent Gautama the Buddha eluding his realm by passing to Nirvāna, from the 'conditioned' to the 'unconditioned' state.

The story is told with much elaborate detail in the Lalita Vistara, an early Sanskrit poem belonging probably to the first century of our era. The fixing of the date of this poem is most important, as many of the so-called parallels between the Buddhist and the Christian stories are drawn from this source. Professor Rhys Davids compares the Lalita Vistara to the Paradise poems of Milton, . e. it is not history so much as allegory and legend.

The story goes that Māra and the Sage had a wordy duel as to the relative merit obtained by them: 'What evidence is there, O Siddartha,' asked the Evil One, 'that you have given alms?' Whereupon the Sage called upon the earth to bear him witness, and she replied with a roar so terrible that even Māra's war-elephant, Mountain-girdled, fell at the Sage's feet.

The Buddhist estimate of the relative worth of the Buddha and the gods is brought out in the account of Māra's onslaught, which was so terrible that the gods in attendance upon the Buddha fled in dismay, whilst the Sage sat unmoved.

II

By patience and tranquillity
(Such was his chosen panoply)
The Sage achieved the victory.
Alāvaka, the demon dread,

The livelong night he combated,
With heart of brass redoubtable
Fiercer than Māra, lord of hell!
  Be yours his glorious victory,
  And yours its ample blessing be!

The story goes that in the sixteenth year of Gautama's Buddhahood, Alāvaka, a demon who used to devour children, appeared before his retreat, and thrice ordered him to come out and go in again. He obeyed patiently and calmly, and then at last refused, whereupon the demon threatened that, if the Sage failed to answer some riddles he would put to him, his head would be broken and his body cast into the Ganges. (See No. VIII above.)

III

By compassion flowing free
He won the glorious victory
O'er elephant Nalāgiri!
As the dreadful thunder crashing,
As the lurid lightning flashing,
As the jungle-fire encroaching,
He beheld the brute approaching.
  Be yours his glorious victory,
  And yours its ample blessing be!

This stanza commemorates the last of the murderous attempts of Devadatta, the cousin and would-be supplanter of the Buddha. In mad jealousy of Gautama he plotted with Ajātasatru, who in turn was jealous of King Bimbisāra: each was to murder his kinsman and to succeed to his office. Ajātasatru succeeded in supplanting Bimbisāra, who retired in his favour, but Devadatta failed either to kill the Buddha or to force him to resign.

'*By compassion flowing free.*' The words refer to the effect of his compassion upon the elephant Nalāgiri, who was in rut, and further maddened by spirits given to him by Devadatta. The brute, on beholding the Sage, fell at his feet and with his trunk removed the dust from them and scattered it over his own head.

IV

By his wondrous magic power,
Stood he as a mighty tower,
In a still more fearsome hour.
Angulimāla, bandit dread
With human fingers garlanded,
Trophies of his victims dead—
Him too the Sage discomfited.
  Be yours his glorious victory,
  And yours its ample blessing be!

Angulimāla was a notorious robber of Kosala who had vowed a garland of 1,000 human fingers, one from each of his victims, as an offering to his tree-god. The Buddha heard of him and sought him out. At first the robber—who had piled up 999 out of the 1,000 fingers he wanted—tried to complete the vow by killing Gautama, but he was soon converted and became an Arahat, so escaping the punishment of his murderous career!

To-day, in Ceylon, Siam, and other Buddhist lands, the following stanza, known as 'Angulimāla's Pirit', is recited over pregnant women to ensure a painless delivery:

'Since I was numbered in the noble company
Of Arahats, no life I've taken willingly.'

V

By peace and self-control serene
Was the mighty Sage victorious seen,
(A glorious victory, I ween!)
When Chincha, feigning pregnancy,
Accused him of unchastity,
And sland'rous lying rumours woke,
Amongst the simple country-folk.
  Be yours his glorious victory,
  And yours its ample blessings be!

A heretical sect, jealous of the Sage, persuaded a lay devotee of their sect, the girl Chincha, to frequent the neighbourhood of his retreat and finally to feign pregnancy and accuse him of being the author of her shame. She tied a heavy wooden bowl beneath her garments, and one day appeared as he was preaching, and before all the people reviled him as her seducer. 'Sister,' he replied with serene calmness, 'no one save only thou and I can tell if these words be false or true.' But though he had forgotten the gods they did not forsake him. For Indra and four attendant gods, veritable *dei ex machina*, appeared in the semblance of mice, ran up her skirts and gnawed the strings by which the bowl was fastened. She disappeared in a flame of fire, and descended to the Avīci-hell.

The gods are conceived in this legend as unseen witnesses of the affairs of men, and able on occasion to interfere on their behalf.

VI

By wisdom's piercing levin-flash,
False Sachcha too did he abash,
And all his trumpery weapons smash:
With envious heart of enmity,
And blinded with perversity,
He came against the mighty Sage
And sought with lies the war to wage.
Be yours his glorious victory,
And yours its ample blessing be!

Sachcha was a false teacher whom the Buddha overthrew.

VII

His pupil too by magic might
Did aid him in the heroic fight,
And put the dreadful snakes to flight:
The Sage's spiritual son,
In serpent's guise, the victory won,
Prevailing by his magic power
O'er demons twain in that dread hour.
Be yours his glorious victory,
And yours its ample blessing be!

Two demons, Nando and Upanando, using magic powers and appearing in the guise of serpents, used to work great havoc amongst the people till Moggallana, one of Gautama's chief disciples, himself assuming the guise of a serpent, put them to flight.

The Arahat has power to assume other forms and to pass through the air unseen to great distances.

VIII

By knowledge did the mighty Sage
(Such was the warfare he did wage)
Bako, the Brahmā god, engage ;
A god was he of power and light,
But poisoned by the envenomed bite
Of the sharp fang of wrong belief ;
In wisdom's drug he found relief !
  Be yours his glorious victory,
  And yours its ample blessing be !

This is one of many passages in which Gautama is depicted as a physician of the soul, curing those who are mentally sick. In this case he cures a heretical god !

Whoso is wise, with wakeful mind alert
Shall say these victory-blessings constantly :
So shall he every threatening ill avert
And tranquil come to Happy Freedom presently.

Note

This poem is of especial value to the student of religions, for it shows how the modern Buddhist thinks of the Buddha, and how the doctrine of 'reversible merit'—that the world to-day can share the merit of Gautama Buddha—has established itself.* Here is the link between the stoicism of primitive Buddhism and the Amida-worship of Japan. May it not also prove a step from the

* Cf. LI.

dim longings of the Buddhist heart for a Saviour to the sure knowledge of salvation in Christ ?

'Long years Thy shadow, brooding o'er these lands,
Hath told of Peace and Hope for sinful men ;
Now turn the Shadow to Reality,
And bless us as we gather round Thy Feet,
Oh ! Amitabha-Christ, sole Lord of All ! '

XLIII

PROOFS OF THE BUDDHA'S EXISTENCE

(Milinda Pañha, 345–7.)

This poem, probably of early post-Christian composition, together with the monuments, provides an effective reply to those critics who have sought to find the origin of the Buddha legends in a Sun-Myth.

As men who see a city fitly planned
Infer the greatness of its architect,
So when the ' City of Good Law ' is scanned
Work of the Blessed One can those who will detect.

As men who see the ocean rollers break
Infer the greatness of th' encompassing sea,
So may they judge of him whose teachings take
Throughout the listening world their course of victory.

Of him, the Victor who allays all grief
Who purged his heart of Tanhā, seed of woe,*
Well may the men to whom he brings relief
Cry, ' Great our Master, far his goodly precepts flow ! '

* See p. 10.

As men who see far-off Himālaya's snows
Can judge the mountain-barriers' soaring height :
So they on whom the Teacher peace bestows
Behold the 'Mount of Dharma' gleaming clear
and white,

Steadfast, unshaken, towering on high,
Unmoved by all the passion-blasts of lust,
In air serene, where ill and Karma die,
Infer 'How great the Hero in whose word we
trust!'

As those who find some track of elephant
Infer the vastness of his kingly form,
So when they see the work of Bhagavant,*
'How mighty', cry they, 'was the Teacher of the
Norm!'

As men behold the jungle-folk afraid
And know 'The King of beasts is surely near',
So when false teachers fly, and are dismayed,
We judge ''Tis wisdom of the royal Sage they fear!'

And when the earth rejoices fresh and green,
'The gracious rain', we say, 'hath come at last.'
So judge we, when the hearts of weary men
Rejoice, 'His gracious words into their lives have
passed.'

Seeing the wide fields turned into a flood,
'Some mighty stream hath poured its waters here,'
Men cry : so judge they of the Law how good
It is, because they see men here and everywhere

* The regular title for Gautama, *The Blessed One.*

In the wide ocean of its waters pure,
Cleansed from the mud of sin and suffering.
As men who scent the fragrant air are sure
That the great forest trees hard-by are blossoming ;

So, finding righteous actions wafting round
All the sweet fragrance of their loveliness,
Men gladly sniff the air, and cries resound,
'Here surely lived a Buddha, Lord of Righteousness!'

XLIV

THE TALE OF THE OGRESS KĀLĪ

(TRANSLATED BY PROFESSOR CHARLES DUROISELLE)

Never through hate can hatreds cease ;
Love only ends them, evermore :
Love only brings all strife to peace ;
Such is the true, the ancient lore.

'NEVER through Hate.' This story did the Master tell what time he dwelt at the Jetavana, about a childless woman.

'Tis said that a certain householder's son, after his father's death, managed by himself the whole of his domestic concerns ; alike in the fields and in the house he worked, taking tender care of his mother. One day his mother said to him :

'I will find thee a maiden (as a wife to thee).'

'Mother,' replied the youth, 'do not speak thus ; so long as my life lasts I will cherish thee alone.'

'Son,' said the mother, 'I am not happy thus, seeing that thou hast now to work both in the fields and in the house ; let me find thee a wife.'

The son, having again and again refused this offer, at the last was silent ; whereupon the mother, having in mind a certain family (in which there was a marriageable daughter), left the house. He asked her :

'To what family dost thou go ?'

But, learning from her 'Such-and-such a family', he dissuaded her ; and indicated the family he himself preferred. Thither she went, asked for the hand of their daughter, fixed the day (for the wedding), and took her home.

Time passed, and the young wife bore no child, seeing which the mother said to the young man :

'My son, the maiden of thine own choice did I bring to our home; and lo! she is without offspring. A sonless family falls into ruin, the line of its succession lost; let me seek out another maiden!'

'Enough! my mother!' he replied; but notwithstanding this she again and again brought up the subject. The childless wife, hearing of this, bethought her: 'Sons verily cannot transgress the commands of their parents; sooner or later they will bring into our home a maiden that will bear a child and will use me as a slave. How, now, if I were to go and myself seek for such a one?' Going to a certain family she asked the daughter of them in marriage to her husband.

'But how, madam, can *you* ask this?' they inquired.

'I am childless, and verily a childless family goes to ruin. Your daughter, having borne a son, will become the mistress of the property.' And, obtaining their consent, she herself took the maiden to her husband's home.

But presently she bethought her: 'If this maiden shall bear either a son or a daughter, she will become the mistress of the property. It behoves me so to act that she bears no child.' Whereupon she told the other:

'When thou knowest thou shalt become a mother, make me acquainted with the fact.' The other assented, and, later, finding she was in the way of motherhood, informed the first wife of the matter. Now the childless woman was wont herself to serve the other with her food; and, learning this, she placed in the younger's rice a potent poison, so that no child was born. Even a second time did matters follow the same course. The neighbouring matrons asked of the young wife :

'Think you some enemy is against you ?' And she told them what had occurred.

'Foolish girl!' cried they, 'wherefore didst thou give her information? Through fear that thou shouldst become mistress has she wronged thee! On no account tell her aught again.'

Thus warned, on the third occasion she said naught to the elder wife. But the latter, later understanding, asked her :

'Why didst thou not acquaint me ?'

'Wherefore, indeed, should I inform thee,' replied the younger, 'seeing that twice thou hast brought me to harm ?'

The childless woman thought, 'Now am I undone!' But, watching for her opportunity in the other's carelessness, she at last, when the time of motherhood was nigh, administered again and again her poison. Because of the advanced progress of the matter, the poison acted not as formerly; and the young mother, in danger of death and suffering the most terrible pain, made this act of resolve concerning the elder wife: 'I, woe is me, am undone! Brought hither by thyself, these three times hast thou slain my offspring, and now am I myself about to die. May I, passing hence, take re-birth as an Ogress,* and may I have power in future lives always to devour thy children.' So resolving, she died, in that very household, and took re-birth in the form of a Cat.†

* Yakkhinī. The Yakkhas are an order of beings gifted with various magical powers, and commonly supposed to feed mainly on human or other flesh.

† Buddhist psychology teaches that the particular

The householder, seizing the childless woman, reproaching her with being the cause of destroying the succession of his family, maltreated her so terribly, beating her with elbows and knees that she died; and she also in that same house took re-birth in the shape of a Hen. The Hen laid eggs, and the Cat devoured them; and so a second, and yet again for the third time. On this last occasion the Hen, perceiving 'Now will this Cat devour me also,' formed the resolve:

'Having died and passed from this existence, may I devour both her and her offspring.'

Dying, she took re-birth as a Panther; and she that was the Cat was re-born as a Doe. Thrice did the Panther come forth and devour the young of that Doe, lastly slaying also the Doe herself. The Doe, at point of death, formed the resolve:

'Thrice have my young been devoured by this Panther; now also will she devour myself. Departing hence, may I in future come to likewise devour her offspring.'

Dying, she was re-born as an Ogress. Later, the Panther herself died, and took re-birth as the daughter of a noble family in Sāvatthi. Coming to maturity, she went to live in her husband's

thought entertained at the moment of death has a special and immediate influence in deciding the Karma, the character of the re-birth taken. In this case the hatred predominant in the woman's mind not only resulted in the achievement of her purpose, but by reason of its intimate association with one of the three forms of Ignorance (Greed, Hatred, and the Delusion of Selfhood) caused her to take re-birth in the Animal World, in the body of an animal in whose nature cruelty, so manifest in the dying woman's wish, plays so predominant a part.

home, in a village hard by the city gate. Time passed by, and she bore a son.

Then the Ogress, taking upon herself the form of a dear friend of that young woman, came to her house and inquired: 'Where is my friend?'

'She rests within, in the inner room; she has become a mother.'

'Is it a son or a daughter?' asked the Ogress; and saying, 'Well, I will go and see,' she entered the inner room; took up the child as if to look at it, and went away. A second time also did the same series of events transpire. The third time the young woman was about to bear offspring she told her husband:

'Beloved, on these two occasions came the Ogress to this house, and devoured both my sons. This time will I go to the house of mine own family.' So saying, she went to her family's house, and in due course became a mother.

Now at that time it chanced to be the turn of the Ogress to carry water. For Kuvera * makes the Ogresses, each in turn, carry for him water from the Anotatta Lake,† passing it from head to head. But our Ogress, so soon as she was relieved from her task, speedily repaired to the young woman's house.

'Where is my friend? Where shall I find her?' asked she.

'In this place an Ogress devours all the sons

* Kuvera, or Vessavana, the King of the Demons, the Guardian of the Eastern quarter of the Heavens, rules over the spirits of the air, and the guardians of treasure.

† Anotatta Lake, one of seven mystical lakes in the Buddhist wonderland, said to be situate amongst the Himalaya Mountains.

that are born unto her; she, therefore, has gone to the house of her own family.'

The Ogress, thinking 'Whithersoever she may go, she shall not escape me', and animated by the depth of her hatred, rushed towards the city.

But the young woman, on the naming day of her child, bathed him; and, a name having been given him, addressed her husband, saying, 'Let us, beloved, now return to our own house.'

Taking her little son, accompanied by her husband, she went along the road. Crossing by the monastery, she gave the babe to him, what time she bathed herself in the pool; and then, whilst her husband bathed, she waited, nursing the child. Suddenly she perceived the Ogress coming; recognizing her, she cried in a loud voice:

'Haste thee; haste thee! O mine husband! This is the Ogress!'

Unable to wait till he could come, she turned back and swiftly ran towards the interior of the monastery.

Now that time, the Teacher was expounding the Dharma in the midst of the congregation. The woman laid the babe at his feet, crying: 'To thee do I make offering of this babe! Save, oh save the life of my child!'

But Sumana, the Deva, who guarded the threshold of the audience hall, did not permit the Ogress to enter. The Master, addressing the Elder Ānanda, said: 'Go thou, Ananda, and call hither this Ogress!'

The Elder called her. The woman, in terror, cried out:

'She comes, Lord! she comes!'

'Let be! Make no disturbance!' was the answer.

And, the Ogress having entered and stood by, the Master said to them :

'Wherefore do ye thus? Had ye not encountered with a Buddha, even as am I, this enmity ye hold one for the other would have endured for the whole period of an aeon ; as did that of the snake and the mongoose ; or that of the crow and the owl. Wherefore do ye thus render back hate for hatred? Hate verily ceaseth by love alone, by hatred never.' And, thus saying, he uttered the stanza :—

Never through hate can hatreds cease ;
Love only ends them, evermore :
Love only brings all strife to peace ;
Such is the true, the ancient lore.

On the recitation of this stanza, the Ogress was established in the fruition of the First Path ; also was this instruction beneficial to all beings assembled. Concluding, the Master said to the woman :

'Give her thy little son!'

'Ah, Lord, I fear to give!' replied the woman.

'Naught hast thou now to fear from her,' said the Master. And the woman obeyed. The Ogress fondled it, caressed it, returned it to the mother, and then sat weeping.

'What is this trouble?' asked the Teacher.

'Formerly, Lord, with but difficulty could I obtain food, making a bare livelihood some way or another ; but now how shall I live at all?'

'Have no fear on that matter,' replied the Master, and, addressing the woman, he said :

'Take her with thee to thy house ; lodge her, and feed her with the rice and gruel first drawn out of the dish.' *

* This is a mark of respect ; the custom still obtains in

The woman took home with her the Ogress; settled her on the cross-beam of the roof, and ministered to her as commanded. But when they pounded the paddy, it seemed to that Ogress as if her head were being battered by pestles. The Ogress, addressing her own friend, said: 'I shall not be able to dwell in this place; let me abide elsewhere.' She was then accommodated in the hut wherein the pestles were kept, in the drinking-water stand, in the kitchen, at the extreme end of the eaves, on the rubbish-heap, and at the village gate, successively. But all these, one after the other, she rejected, saying:

'Here it is as though my head were broken with pounding; there at the water-stand, the children throw in my direction the water with which they have cleansed their hands or rinsed their mouths; in the kitchen dogs come to sleep; on the ground below the end of the eaves there are impurities; on the rubbish-heap sweepings are cast; and at the village-gate boys shoot as at a target.' Finally they put her in a solitary place without the village; and thither brought to her the rice first drawn from the dish. So she lived satisfied, and was wont to tell her friend (that for so many lives had followed her as enemy): 'This year the rains will be good; sow on high ground your seed. This year the rains will be little; sow on low-lying ground.' Thus it happened that her crops always succeeded well; whilst those of others were spoilt, betimes by overmuch water and betimes by drought. The villagers, seeing this, asked her on what account

the East. Elders, parents, or guests must serve themselves, or be served, first. An infringement of this rule is considered a gross breach of etiquette.

it was that her crops were always successful, and in what fashion she knew that the rains each year would be good or bad, and sowed accordingly. She replied: 'Thus are we instructed by the Ogress, and, attending to her words, we sow, betimes on low land and betimes on high; thus is it that our crops are always a success. Have you not seen that the first of everything is carried to her from our house? You, likewise, do the same; and she will also take interest in your work.'

Thenceforward the villagers made offerings to the Ogress; who, in return, advised them as to their domestic concerns; thus she constantly was in receipt of the best of gifts, and found many adherents. She it was who, subsequently, instituted the system of issuing tickets for the distribution of the eight kinds of food; and this system is in vogue, even to this day.

XLV

THE STORY OF PRINCE WESSANTARA

Prince Wessantara was the son of Visvamitta, and is described as ideally handsome according to Indian standards: 'his complexion golden, his brow like a dome, his arms long, his eyebrows meeting, and his nose aquiline'. He was as good as he was beautiful, and so liberal in giving that his father in a rage banished him from his kingdom.

The story of his wonderful self-effacement is very popular in Buddhist lands, forming the subject of frescoes on the temple walls, and the subject of never-ending comment.

The following is a paraphrase which keeps close to the original, but is condensed for the sake of brevity.

BEING banished by his father, Wessantara the Bodhisat went to his wife Maddi and told her that he had vowed to go out into the jungle and lead the solitary life of contemplation. 'I too will come with my lord,' said the faithful wife: 'how can I live parted from thee for a moment? As the moonless sky, as the waterless earth, so is a wife without her husband.'

So they went out together into the jungle.

After some days a Brahman approached and asked that the prince should give him his splendid chariot; and when the Princess Maddi grew angry at his request the prince rebuked her, saying, 'O Maddi, if there were none to make requests there would be no giving; whence then should we mortals gain the true insight that comes only to the liberal?' and with great joy he gave both chariot and horses to the Brahman, exclaiming, 'O Brahman, through this gift freely given, may I be empowered to guide the chariot of the Righteous Law!'

Then taking up their children Jaliya and Krishnayina upon their shoulders, they passed on their way.

One day, whilst the Princess was out gathering roots and wild fruits for their evening meal, a hunchbacked Brahman drew near and addressed the Prince, 'O Prince of the Kshatriya stock, all hail! No servant have I, and alone I wander through the jungle. Give me, I pray thee, thy children.' And when Wessantara hesitated, he reminded him of his name for liberality and adjured him to live worthy of it. Wessantara thereupon laying aside the yearning of his heart, reasoned with himself, 'If now I give the children to the Brahman, then will Maddi and I feel the cruel pain of bereavement: but if I give them not

I shall prove faithless to my vow, and the Brahman will be disappointed of his hope.' He reflected further that these sufferings were coming upon him that he might in due season become the Enlightened and save from the ocean of ignorance those who are sinking in its bottomless depths.

So he gave the children to the Brahman. Whereupon the earth quaked six times ; and the children fell at their father's feet crying, 'O father, let us but see our mother e'er we leave you both for ever.' And the Prince, covering his face with his hand to hide his tears, said in a breaking voice, 'O my children, in my heart is no harshness, only boundless compassion. I give you away that I may attain perfect insight.'

And they, with hands placed palm to palm, laid their heads upon his feet and prayed for forgiveness of all their faults ; and so went forth. And he, as they looked back and ever turned to look one long last look, consoled them with compassionate words.

Then, desiring perfect insight, he entered alone into his hut of leaves.

The air straightway was filled with cries of legions of gods exclaiming, 'O, the great deed of sacrifice! Wondrous is he whose mind is unshaken even at the loss of both his children!'

Then Maddi the mother drew near, and her heart was full of foreboding as she saw the little house they had built of mud, and all their playthings lying deserted: weeping she threw herself at her husband's feet, and asked him of them. And he made answer, 'Rejoice, my wife! A Brahman came and asked me for them, and I gave them to him.' As a stricken hart, she fell at his feet and lay as a fish that breathes out its life upon the shore: and as a cow robbed of her calf she mourned: 'As young tender lilies my children suffer: as young gazelles snared by the huntsman are they dwelling with strangers. They whom I nourished at these breasts are now in the hands of sinful men; hungry and thirsty they cry for me in despair. O miserable woman! What dreadful sin have I sinned that this suffering has overtaken me?'

And she called upon the trees that they had watered and upon their playmates the gazelles to witness the dreadful torments of her heart.

But the Bodhisat comforted her and exhorted her to be strong: and she came to herself at length and said: 'I will not be a hindrance to you, O my husband! If it please you, give me also as a gift.'

Then Sakra, the chief of gods, wondering at the fortitude of Wessantara, thought thus with himself, 'Surely this man, if he be left quite alone, may fail of his endurance,' and taking the form of a Brahman he came to the Bodhisat and addressed him thus: 'Fair is the Princess; blameless wife and peerless among women. Give her to me as my slave.' But Maddi reviled him, 'O man of lust, long not for her who delights only in the law of righteousness.'

Then the Bodhisat; looking upon her with heart of compassion, spoke: 'O wife, I seek after the heights, and I must pass beyond anguish to calm. No lament or complaint must I utter. Do thou therefore go with the Brahman uncomplainingly, and I will live alone in the jungle.'

So saying, he exulted and cried, 'Best of my gifts is this! Take, O Brahman, my dear dear wife; loving and submissive is she in all things.'

Then the earth shook to its foundations, as a boat on a stormy sea: and Sakra, the chief of gods, revealed himself and promised to give the Princess whatever she should wish.

And she, motherlike, besought him that her children might find their way to their grandfather's court. He granted her request, and restored her to the Bodhisat, warning him never again to part with so devoted a wife.

Note

The gods are still subject to frailty, and have not yet reached the heights which are above all feeling! In commenting upon this story to a learned Buddhist, I remarked that the fate of these children was too terrible to be contemplated with equanimity, and that no Western mind could bring itself to believe that Wessantara did well. He replied with a shrug, 'Unless their Karma had brought it upon them, it would not have come to pass.'

XLVI

A BUDDHIST SOLOMON

(Ummagga Jātaka.)

This story is one of a series which show the wisdom of the Bodhisat, or future Buddha. At the age of seven he gave various judgements, of which this is one. The similarity of it to that of the judgement of Solomon inevitably suggests the possibility of borrowing, and this is one of the few cases where it seems quite likely to have occurred. For, as we read, Solomon, whose date is about 1000 B.C., sent ships to get 'ivory, apes, and peacocks', all products of India, and they may well have carried this story with them. It is quite certain that Buddhism did not hesitate to use existing folk-lore to illustrate its teachings, and that the Jātaka Book is very largely composed of such material.

Possibly No. LI also shows traces of Old Testament influence. (Cf. the story of Daniel.)

It is said that a woman carrying her child on her hip went to the tank to bathe, and leaving him lying upon her clothes entered the water. Thereupon straightway an Ogress, seeing the boy and desiring to eat him, took the form of a woman and standing by him called to the mother, 'What a pretty child this is! May I suckle him?' The mother agreed, and the Ogress, taking him up, gave him some milk, and then ran away with him. When the mother seized her she put on a bold face and claimed the child as her own. Now it chanced that, as they wrangled over the child, they passed by the Judgement Hall; and the Bodhisat, hearing their quarrel, sent for them and asked them the cause of the dispute. As he looked upon the Ogress he perceived that her eyes were red as Olinda seeds * and did not blink, and knowing her to be an ogress, he asked, 'Will you be content to abide by my decision?' They agreed, and he bade the attendants draw a line upon the ground, and lay the child upon it exactly in the middle. He then told the ogress to grasp the boy's arms, and the mother to grasp his legs, and both to pull, until one prevailed and pulled him over the line. 'Whoso wins', he declared, 'shall become the possessor of the child!'

They began to tug and the child to scream with pain; whereat the mother, yearning over him, let

* A beautiful red bean with a black base, much used in Ceylon in a game called 'Olinda'.

go her son and stood lamenting. The Bodhisat turned to those who stood by and asked them, 'Whose heart is pitiful to children, the heart of a mother or the heart of a stranger?' And they answered, 'O wise man! it is the heart of a mother that is tender.' . . . So the mother took her child in her arms and went out saying, 'Long may you live, O master!'

The Ogress took the Five Precepts, and then she too went her way.

XLVII

THE CRUEL CRANE OUTWITTED

(Baka Jātaka.)

(Translated by Professor Rhys Davids in *Buddhist Birth-Stories.*)

The villain though exceeding clever.—This the Master told when at Jetavana about a monk who was a tailor.

There was a monk, says the tradition, living at Jetavana, who was exceeding skilful at all kinds of things that can be done to a robe, whether cutting out, or piecing together, or valuing, or sewing it. Through this cleverness of his he was always engaged in making robes, until he became known as 'The robe-maker'.

Now what used he to do but exercise his handicraft on some old pieces of cloth, so as to make out of them a robe soft and pleasant to the touch; and when he had dyed it, he would steep it in mealy water, and rub it with a chankshell so as to make it bright and attractive, and then lay it carefully by. And monks who did not understand robe work would come to him with new cloths, and say:

'We don't understand how to make robes. Be so kind as to make this into a robe for us.'

Then he would say, 'It takes a long time, Brother, before a robe can be made. But I have a robe ready made. You had better leave these cloths here and take that away with you.'

And he would take it out and show it to them.

And they, seeing of how fine a colour it was, and not noticing any difference, would give their new cloths to the tailor monk, and take the robe away with them, thinking it would last. But when it grew a little dirty, and they washed it in warm water, it would appear as it really was, and the worn-out places would show themselves here and there upon it. Then, too late, they would repent.

And that monk became notorious, as one who passed off old rags upon anybody who came to him.

Now there was another robe-maker in a country village who used to cheat everybody just like the man at Jetavana. And some monks who knew him very well told him about the other, and said to him:

'Sir, there is a monk at Jetavana who, they say, cheats all the world in such and such a manner.'

'Ah!' thought he, ''twould be a capital thing if I could outwit that city fellow!'

And he made a fine robe out of old clothes, dyed it a beautiful red, put it on, and went to Jetavana. As soon as the other saw it, he began to covet it, and asked him:

'Is this robe one of your own making, sir?'

'Certainly, brother,' was the reply.

'Sir! let me have the robe. You can take another for it,' said he.

'But, brother, we village monks are but badly provided. If I give you this, what shall I have to put on?'

'I have some new cloths, sir, by me. Do you take those and make a robe for yourself.'

'Well, brother! this is my own handiwork; but if you talk like that, what can I do? You may have it,' said the other; and giving him the robe made of old rags, he took away the new cloths in triumph.

And the man of Jetavana put on the robe; but when a few days after he discovered, on washing it, that it was made of rags, he was covered with confusion. And it became noised abroad in the Order, 'That Jetavana robe-maker has been outwitted, they say, by a man from the country!'

And one day the monks sat talking about this in the Lecture Hall, when the Teacher came up and asked them what they were talking about, and they told him the whole matter.

Then the Teacher said, 'Not now only has the Jetavana robe-maker taken in other people in this way; in a former birth he did the same. And not now only has he been outwitted by the countryman; in a former birth he was outwitted too.' And he told a tale.

Long ago the Bodhisat was born to a forest life as the Genius of a tree standing near a certain lotus pond.

Now at that time the water used to run short at the dry season in a certain pond, not over large, in which there were a good many fish. And a crane thought, on seeing the fish:

'I must outwit these fish somehow or other, and make a prey of them.'

And he went and sat down at the edge of the water, thinking how he should do it.

When the fish saw him, they asked him, 'What are you sitting there for, lost in thought ?'

'I am sitting thinking about you,' said he.

'O sir, what are you thinking about us ?' said they.

'Why,' he replied, 'there is very little water in this pond, and but little for you to eat; and the heat is so great! So I was thinking, "What in the world will these fish do now ?"'

'Yes, indeed, sir! what *are* we to do ?' said they.

'If you will only do as I bid you, I will take you in my beak to a fine large pond, covered with all the kinds of lotuses, and put you into it,' answered the crane.

'That a crane should take thought for the fishes is a thing unheard of, sir, since the world began. It's eating us, one after the other, that you're aiming at!'

'Not I! So long as you trust me, I won't eat you. But if you don't believe me that there is such a pond, send one of you with me to go and see it.'

Then they trusted him, and handed over to him one of their number—a big fellow, blind of one eye, whom they thought sharp enough in any emergency, afloat or ashore.

Him the crane took with him, let him go in the pond, showed him the whole of it, brought him back, and let him go again close to the other fish. And he told them all the glories of the pond.

And when they heard what he said, they exclaimed, 'All right, sir! You may take us with you.'

Then the crane took the old purblind fish first to the bank of the other pond, and alighted in a Varana-tree growing on the bank there. But he threw it into a fork of the tree, struck it with his beak, and killed it; and then ate its flesh, and threw its bones away at the foot of the tree. Then he went back and called out:

'I have thrown that fish in; let another come!'

And in that manner he took all the fish, one by one, and ate them, till he came back and found no more!

But there was still a crab left behind there; and the crane thought he would eat him too, and called out:

'I say, good crab, I've taken all the fish away, and put them into a fine large pond. Come along. I'll take you too!'

'But how will you take hold of me to carry me along?'

'I'll bite hold of you with my beak.'

'You'll let me fall if you carry me like that. I won't go with you!'

'Don't be afraid! I'll hold you quite tight all the way.'

Then said the crab to himself, 'If this fellow once got hold of fish, he would never let them go in a pond! Now if he should really put me into the pond, it would be capital; but if he doesn't—then I'll cut his throat, and kill him!' So he said to him:

'Look here, friend, you won't be able to hold me tight enough; but we crabs have a famous grip.

If you let me catch hold of you round the neck with my claws, I shall be glad to go with you.'

And the other did not see that he was trying to outwit him, and agreed. So the crab caught hold of his neck with his claws as securely as with a pair of blacksmith's pincers, and called out, 'Off with you, now!'

And the crane took him and showed him the pond, and then turned off towards the Varana-tree.

'Uncle!' cried the crab, 'the pond lies that way, but you are taking me this way!'

'Oh, that's it, is it!' answered the crane. 'Your dear little uncle, my very sweet nephew, you call me! You mean me to understand, I suppose, that I am your slave, who has to lift you up and carry you about with him! Now cast your eye upon the heap of fish-bones lying at the root of yonder Varana-tree. Just as I have eaten those fish, every one of them, just so I will devour you as well!'

'Ah! those fishes got eaten through their own stupidity,' answered the crab; 'but I'm not going to let you eat *me*. On the contrary, it is *you* that I am going to destroy. For you in your folly have not seen that I was outwitting you. If we die, we die both together; for I will cut off this head of yours, and cast it to the ground!' And so saying, he gave the crane's neck a grip with his claws, as with a vice.

Then gasping, and with tears trickling from his eyes, and trembling with the fear of death, the crane besought him, saying, 'O my Lord! Indeed I did not intend to eat you. Grant me my life!'

'Well, well! step down into the pond, and put me in there.'

And he turned round and stepped down into the pond, and placed the crab on the mud at its edge. But the crab cut through its neck as clean as one would cut a lotus-stalk with a hunting-knife, and then only entered the water!

When the Genius who lived in the Varana-tree saw this strange affair, he made the wood resound with his plaudits, uttering in a pleasant voice the verse:

> 'The villain, though exceeding clever,
> Shall prosper not by his villany.
> He may win, indeed, sharp-witted in deceit,
> But only as the crane here from the crab!'

When the Teacher had finished this discourse, showing that 'Not now only, O mendicants, has this man been outwitted by the country robe-maker, long ago he was outwitted in the same way,' he established the connexion, and summed up the Jataka, by saying, 'At that time he was the Jetavana robe-maker, the crab was the country robe-maker, but the Genius of the Tree was I myself.'

XLVIII

TRUE LOVE

THE STORY OF VISĀHKĀ

(Dhammapada Commentary.)

THE Upasika Visākhā was in the habit of giving alms to the Bhikkhus. One day her grand-daughter Suddata, who lived with her, fell ill and died, and Visākhā, throwing the body into the charnel-pit, was unable to bear the grief. So she betook her to the Buddha and sat on one side sad and tearful. 'O Visākhā!' asked the Blessed One, 'wherefore dost thou sit sad and mournful, shedding tears?' She told him of her granddaughter's death, saying, 'She was a dutiful girl, and I cannot find her like.'

'How many men are there dwelling in Savātthī, O Visākhā?'

'Lord, men say there are seven kotis' (seventy millions).

'If all these were like thy granddaughter, wouldst thou not love them?'

'Verily, Lord.'

'And how many die daily in Savātthī?'

'Many, Lord.'

'Then there is never a moment when thou wouldst not be grieving for some one!'

'True, Master.'

'Wouldst thou then spend thy life weeping day and night?'

'I understand, Lord; it is well said!'

'Grieve then no more.'

Note

This anecdote is told to illustrate the Buddha's teaching as to affection. It is said in the Dhammapada (213), 'From affection come grief and fear. He who is free from affection knows neither grief nor fear.' This is a part of the 'intellectual landscape' of Buddhism which is so strange to Western eyes; and misunderstanding is rife in the writings of Western students, both friendly and hostile. As this story clearly shows, Buddhism teaches benevolence to all, but attachment to none: all are to be equally regarded. The common title for Ānanda in Western books, 'the beloved disciple', is due to an unwarrantable seeking after parallels between the Buddha and the Christ. Gautama would have strongly repudiated the idea that he had any special affection for any one of his disciples. It must be noted that *Pema*, the word here rendered 'affection', is one of the subdivisions of *Tanhā*, that 'desire' which is the root of all evil. The following story, also from the Dhammapada Commentary, and translated by Mr. D. J. Subasinha, illustrates the same point.

XLIX

WRONG LOVE

THE STORY OF GOSĀKA

(Dhammapada, 213.)

(Translated from the Dhammapada Commentary by Mr. D. J. Subasinha.)

IN the town of Kosambi a courtesan gave birth to a child. Knowing that it was a son, she ordered it to be thrown on a dunghill, upon which a crowd of dogs and crows surrounded the child. A neighbour being attracted by the sight, came hither and carried the child home with great affection. A Sitāna (a millionaire) of the town, on his way to the palace, met the royal astrologer returning home, and inquired from him as to the position of the planets on that day. 'Any child born to-day', he said, 'will become the chief Sitāna of the town.'

During the day, his wife was in labour, and he, therefore, being anxious to get home, hastened to the palace and returned. He then ordered a maidservant named Kālī to bring any male child born in the town on that day by giving for it one thousand pieces of money. She went about inquiring, and finding a child born on that day, paid one thousand pieces of money to the parents and brought it to the Sitāna, who thought that if his wife should bring forth a daughter she could be married to this child, but if a son, then this child should be destroyed. His wife gave birth to a son, so he resolved to destroy the other child, and various methods were adopted to carry out his design. This child was first left at the gate of a cattle-shed to be trampled on by the cattle; then it was placed on the high road, to be run over by carts or trampled on by oxen. Again it was left in a cemetery, to be eaten by the Yakkhas (demons), but there it was nursed by a she-goat; and on another occasion it was thrown down a precipice, over which condemned criminals were cast. Each time the Sitāna spent one thousand pieces of money to get back the child from those who had rescued it on the several occasions. The child now began to grow steadily and was named Gosāka.

The Sitāna had a friend, who was a potter by profession, to whom he said, 'Friend, do me the favour of destroying my illegitimate son, by throwing him into your oven, for doing which I now advance you one thousand pieces of money. To-morrow I shall send the boy on to you,' and to this the potter agreed. The following morning the Sitāna summoned Gosāka and said to him, 'Son, I entrusted some work to that potter yesterday, go and tell him to do that work to-day.' Now Gosāka started on this mission, and his brother, who was playing ball, observing him bound on a journey inquired where he was going to, and Gosāka duly informed him; whereupon the brother volunteered to undertake the work, and in turn told Gosāka to make up whatever he had lost in playing. At first Gosāka disliked the idea, but on his brother insisting, Gosāka remained playing and his brother went on the errand. When the brother met the potter, the latter took him up and threw him into the oven.

Some time afterwards Gosāka went home and the Sitāna asked him whether he had gone to the potter; and being informed of what had happened, immediately went running to the potter, only to be told that he had done as he had promised him. The Sitāna was overwhelmed with grief, and passed his days in great misery. The Sitāna committed these crimes owing to the affection he bore towards his own son.

L

THE PROBLEM OF SUFFERING

'As a man soweth, so shall he reap.'

(Milinda Pañha, 111.[42])

THUS spake King Milinda: 'How comes it, reverend sir, that men are not alike? Some live long, and some are short-lived; some are hale, and some weak; some comely, and some ugly; some powerful, and some with no power; some rich, some poor; some born of noble stock, some meanly born; some wise, and some foolish.'

To whom Nāgasena the Elder made answer:

'How comes it that all plants are not alike? Some have a sour taste and some are salt, some are acid, some acrid, some bitter, and some sweet.'

'It must be, I take it, reverend sir, that they spring from various kinds of seed.'

'Even so, O Mahārāja, it is because of differences of action that men are not alike: for some live long, and some are short-lived; some are hale, and some weak; some comely, and some ugly; some powerful, and some without power; some rich, some poor; some born of noble stock, some meanly born; some wise, and some foolish.'

LI

THE POWER OF THE NORM

In olden times there lived in the town of Kosambi a very pious king, whose queen Wessamitta was very dear to him. She was a devoted adherent of the Triple Gem, and faithfully kept the Five Precepts. Now when an enemy invaded his kingdom, and he was setting out with his fourfold army to meet him, Wessamitta would fain accompany him.

The King sought to dissuade her, for she was great with child; but she would not hearken, and at last he yielded and took her with him. But before he went on to the field of battle he placed her in safety, and bade his men if he were defeated to hoist a red flag, that she might take warning and escape.

The battle lasted long, and he was slain; and the Queen, seeing the red flag, began to wail and lament. Thus the spies of the enemy captured her and brought her to their lord. And he, seeing her beauty, was enamoured of her and would fain have made her his. But she, who dearly loved her dead lord, would not consent. In various ways he tempted her, and at last sought by terror to win her consent.

When she remained steadfast he bade them throw her into a pit of fire; but she besought him in these words to have pity:

'It was said, O King, by them of old time that to slay holy men, Brahmans, parents, children, the sick or women, is a deed which no man praises. Therefore slay me not.'

But the King was the more enraged, and bade

his men carry out his orders. And she, cherishing no idea of vengeance or of hatred towards her enemy, began to meditate upon the qualities of the Three Refuges and the Five Precepts. And by their power it came to pass that the fire which raged all round her seemed like a pool of cold water in summer, soothing and cool.

The King, moved to repentance, lifted her out of the flames, and she uttered the following stanza :

> The Buddha have I taken as my fortress ;
> He alone hath been my mighty tower ;
> Trusting midst the raging of the furnace
> I was rescued by his all-availing power.

And she taught him of the fruits of the Five Precepts and of the Three Refuges, how by their power she remained calm even in the midst of the flames : 'No other charms I had to protect me.'

And he rejoiced and took the Three Refuges and the Five Precepts, and restored the Queen to her own kingdom.

LII

DO THE DEAD MEET AGAIN ?

The Story of Nokula's Father

(Anguttara Nikāya, IV.[1])

Once the Blessed One was dwelling amongst the Bhaggas on the Peak of Sumsumaro in the Bhesakala Garden of the Deer Park ; and taking his robe and bowl, he came to the home of Nokula's father, and sat him down upon the seat they had prepared for him. Then the good man of the house, Nokula's father, came with his wife to the Blessed One, and sitting on one side, addressed him thus: 'O sir, the mother of Nokula came at a very tender age to my home. And since that day, she has not, I think, been unfaithful to me even in thought. I would be with her in the next life as well as in this.'

And the mother of Nokula also came to the Blessed One and said, 'O sir, since I was brought as a very young wife to the house of Nokula's father he has not, I think, been unfaithful to me even in thought. I would fain be his in the next life as in this.'

Then the Blessed One spoke: 'If man and wife wish to be together in the next life as in this, let them be peers in faith, peers in morality, and peers in liberality and wisdom: then shall they meet in the next life.

When man and wife are peers in chastity,
In faith and righteousness and charity,
When each the other serveth lovingly,
Then shall they dwell in bliss and health.
Their foes shall grieve to see their wealth:
And since in all things they are peers
Rebirth in heavenly realms is theirs,
And gladly each with other shares
The bliss they've won in lower spheres!'

Note

This is a question which naturally exercises the mind of Buddhists, and the chances of re-union are, according to this teaching, so slender that the most orthodox believer is often a heretic in this one respect. When we reflect that it is the common belief that a good woman will be reborn as a man, it will be seen how far the teaching here given is from satisfying the craving of their hearts. Nevertheless, they would account for the phenomenon of 'love at first sight' in this way: the lovers were together in a former birth, and when Karma brings about a meeting each instinctively recognizes the beloved, though outward forms have changed.

The Christian doctrine of a Heaven where there is a 'knitting up of sundered ties' attracts Buddhists very powerfully, and many of them have taken it over into their religion.

LIII

THE LAYMAN'S PART

(Vyaggapajja Sutta.)

(Translated by Mr. D. J. Subasinha.)

Thus I (Ānanda) heard.

Once the Blessed One was residing among the Kôliyans at Kakkarapattam, a village in the territory of the Kôliyan King.

Now at that time a Kôliyan named Dhîgâjanu (Longshanks) went to where the Blessed One was, and having paid due obeisance to Him, sat down on one side. Being thus seated, the Kôliyan named Dhîgâjanu addressed the Blessed One thus:

'Venerable Lord, as laymen we pass our days enjoying the five sensual pleasures; and on account of the maintenance of our wives and children we do not find sufficient time to devote to the performance of meritorious deeds. We perfume our bodies with sandal-wood grown in the country called Kâsi and with different other odours. We adorn our bodies with garlands of beautiful and fragrant flowers of different varieties. We anoint our bodies with sweet-scented unguents. We possess gold and silver, and we enrich our bodies with ornaments made of gold and embossed with pearls and jewels.

'Venerable Lord, if there be a doctrine which

will be of use to us as laymen, and which will conduce to our welfare in this world, and for our happiness in the world to come, pray declare unto us that doctrine.'

The Lord spoke and said: 'Vyaggapajja, by the observation of these four doctrines the layman will be enabled to lead a virtuous life in this world, and in the life hereafter enjoy a happy life. What are these four?

'They are:

1. Perseverance.
2. Protection of wealth.
3. True friendship.
4. Frugality.

'What, O Vyaggapajja, is perseverance? In this world, Vyaggapajja, whatever profession a layman may pursue for his sustenance, be it either agriculture, or commerce, or cattle-farming, or fencing, or statesmanship, or any other profession, such as smithy and pottery, and gain his livelihood by being efficient in these arts, and unremitting in his endeavours, and if he watch the right time to do a piece of work and do it at the proper time, or without sloth if he cause the work to be done at the proper time and supervise it, he judges and acts wisely. Acquisition of wealth or achievement of success, O Vyaggapajja, by persistent effort and unremitting energy in this manner, is called perseverance.

'What, O Vyaggapajja, is protection of wealth? Vyaggapajja, a layman may have wealth acquired by constant diligence, by the strength of his limbs, by the sweat of his brow, by well-concerted plans, and by right means of livelihood. One shall then consider: this wealth acquired by me I shall protect from burglars, protect from danger arising by fire, protect from inundations, protect from danger arising from authorities, and protect from disagreeable and jealous relatives. The taking care of wealth acquired with difficulty in this manner, Vyaggapajja, is called protection.

'What, Vyaggapajja, is true friendship? In this world, Vyaggapajja, if a householder, living in a village or hamlet, find there a householder or his son, who is a strict observer of the precepts (Dharma), has cultivated his intellect, is spiritually developed, is firm in faith, performs duties devolving on laymen, is liberally disposed towards others, has a profound acquaintance with different sciences, and if he associate with the householder or his son as above described, discuss with him, converse with him, that householder will become a strict observer of the precepts, cultivate his intellect, develop spiritually, be firm in faith, perform duties devolving upon laymen, be liberally disposed towards others, acquire a profound knowledge of the sciences, and do all that is good, and refrain from all that is bad. This, Vyaggapajja, is called true friendship.

'What, Vyaggapajja, is frugality? In this world, Vyaggapajja, if a householder, considering wisely and realizing the difficulty of acquiring wealth and the manner in which the wealth so acquired should be spent, be moderate in his expenses, that is, earn twice as much as is spent, and neither spend too much, nor spend too little, then the wealth so acquired will not be wasted, but be preserved.

'Vyaggapajja, as a trader or his subordinate uses a balance and perceives that when a weight is introduced to a scale pan that one side is lowered owing to excess of weight, while the other is raised owing to the want of an equal weight; in like manner the householder should understand well the extent of his income and spend proportionate to his means, considering the difficulty of acquiring wealth and the impropriety of spending it lavishly. He should spend economically according to his means and sustain himself. In this manner a householder should refrain from extravagance, and be economical in his expenses. Then his earnings will not be wasted, but be preserved.

'Vyaggapajja, a householder who earns little but spends beyond his means is compared unto a man, who, desirous of eating wood-apple, climbs up a tree, shakes the branches, letting both the ripe and unripe fruits fall down, collects them, eats the ripe fruits, and throws aside the unripe ones. People will readily deprecate such wastage.

'Vyaggapajja, if a householder be miserly, making no proper use of his earnings, and die, he will be subjected to blame, in not having spent them during his lifetime for what was worthy.

'Vyaggapajja, in this manner a householder should wisely consider the difficulty of acquiring wealth and the impropriety of spending beyond his means the wealth acquired by .persistent efforts. He should consider in this wise, 'This wealth acquired by me I shall not spend lavishly, but spend it economically and solely for my wants.' The spending of wealth in this manner, Vyaggapajja, is called frugality.

'Vyaggapajja, there are four ways in which the

wealth lawfully acquired by indefatigable energy is liable to be destroyed. What are these four ways? They are:

1. Indulgence in unlawful sexual intercourse.
2. Indulgence in the use of intoxicating liquors.
3. Indulgence in gambling.
4. Indulgence in associating with unrighteous friends.

'Vyaggapajja, if a lake, well fortified by embankments, has four feeding streams, and four outlets; and if the four inlets be blocked, and the passage of the four outlets be cleared up by the removal of silt to facilitate the outflow of water, and if there be no currents of air to obstruct the movement of water, the water in the lake will gradually flow out and the lake will be emptied. In like manner, Vyaggapajja, will the wealth of a man be destroyed, who indulges in unlawful sexual intercourse, indulges in the use of intoxicating liquors, indulges in gambling, and indulges in the association of unrighteous friends, such as joining vicious men in the time of their prosperity and moving in their society.

'Vyaggapajja, there are four ways in which the wealth acquired by persistent efforts may be increased and saved. What are these four? They are (1) refraining from the indulgence in unlawful sexual intercourse, (2) refraining from the indulgence in the use of intoxicating liquors, (3) refraining from the indulgence in gambling, (4) the association with righteous men. These are the four ways tending to the increase of wealth.

'Vyaggapajja, if a lake, well fortified by embankments, has four feeding streams and four outlets, and if the four outlets be blocked up, and the passage of the four inlets be cleared up by the removal of silt to facilitate the influx of water, and if there be no current of air to obstruct the inward flow of water, the water of the lake will not be diminished, but be gradually increased, and consequently the lake will be full.

'In the same manner, Vyaggapajja, will the wealth of a man be increased who refrains from indulgence in unlawful sexual intercourse, indulgence in the use of intoxicating liquors, indulgence in gambling, indulgence in associating with unrighteous men. Vyaggapajja, by the observation of these four principles will the layman be enabled to lead a virtuous life in this world, and be happy in the world to come.

'Vyaggapajja, adherence to the following four principles will enable a layman to attain a good birth in the world to come, and enjoy heavenly bliss. What are these four ? (1) Faith, (2) Observation of the precepts, (3) Liberality, (4) Prudence.

'What, O Vyaggapajja, is faith ? If in this world, Vyaggapajja, a layman have faith, he will repose confidence in the sublime wisdom of Lord Buddha. Thinking in this manner will he repose confidence : 'Lord Buddha has overcome all sins. He has by self-exertion fully comprehended the cause of all things. He has kind words for all, and his actions are actuated by infinite love towards mankind. He understands all about the world. He causes men to refrain from sin and sets them on the right path. He is the adviser of the Devas and of all mankind. He discovered the four Noble Truths and expounded those doctrines to others. He has subjugated all kinds of passions and killed desire.' Reposing confidence in this manner on the sublime wisdom of Lord Buddha, Vyaggapajja, is called faith.*

'What, O Vyaggapajja, is meant by the observation of the precepts? If in this world, Vyaggapajja, a layman refrain from destroying life, refrain from taking that which is not given, refrain from unlawful sexual intercourse, refrain from the use of intoxicating liquors, this is called the observation of the precepts.

'What, O Vyaggapajja, is liberality? If in this world a layman would, by insatiate desire and selfishness, envy others' wealth and consider, 'May this wealth of mine not pass away unto others,' that is not liberality. But if he have a compassionate heart towards others and be ready to give unto others proportionate to his means, and if he give unto others when demanded and make others to partake of his riches, that, Vyaggapajja, is called liberality.

'What, O Vyaggapajja, is prudence? If in this world, Vyaggapajja, a layman dispels ignorance, which stands in the way of one's spiritual development, or the achievement of success in this world, and acquire enlightenment, and ponder over the dissolution of the Skandhas, by the conjunction of which man is constituted, and the subjection of everything in this world to impermanence, this, Vyaggapajja, is called prudence.

'Vyaggapajja, by the observation of these four principles will laymen be enabled to attain a good birth in the world to come, and enjoy heavenly bliss.'

* Faith in Buddhism is reliance upon the system expounded by Gautama: Faith in Christianity is trust in a Person.

After the Blessed One had preached unto Vyaggapajja in this manner, treating about the principles, the observance of which will tend to bring happiness in this world and in the world to come hereafter, he again uttered the following concisely in verses (Gāthās):

'That layman knows no sinful thought,
Who does with promptness what he ought,
Protects his wealth with prudent care,
Yet gives away a fitting share;
And, full of faith in Buddha's Law,
Holds to its precepts fast and sure.
Thus frugal, prudent, liberal he
By Faith and Zeal shall sinless be;
Thus happy here he lives below,
And later glad to heaven shall go.'

Note

It will be noticed that the Goal here set before the laity is not Nirvāna, which does not attract them, but a Heaven of Bliss, which does. The question 'How can we even achieve this much of the Eightfold Path?' greatly exercises the earnest Buddhist; and in practice he prays and makes offerings that he may be reborn in this world when Maitri, or Metteyya, the next Buddha, comes. That this 'Loving One' has already come, and will return, it is the privilege of the missionary to proclaim.

THE END